T0356502

THE
CHAMPION'S
CREED

BEN UTECHT

SUPER BOWL CHAMPION & CHIEF CULTURE OFFICER

THE
CHAMPION'S
CREED

TRANSFORM YOUR CULTURE THROUGH
THE POWER OF BELIEF

PREFACE BY TONY DUNGY

WILEY

Library of Congress Cataloging-in-Publication Data is available:

ISBN: 9781394331239 (cloth)
ISBN: 9781394331246 (ePub)
ISBN: 9781394331253 (ePDF)

Cover Design: Wiley
Cover Image: © dimair/Shutterstock
Author Photo: © Karyn Utecht

SKY10100403_031925

To my wife, Karyn, the anchor of my soul and the light in my storms. Your love, wisdom, and unwavering faith have shaped me into the man I am today. You are my greatest blessing and my truest champion in every season of life.

And to my four beautiful daughters—Elleora, Katriel, Amy, and Haven—you are the culture of my life, filling my days with purpose, joy, and boundless love. Your laughter and light remind me daily of what matters most.

This book is for you—my heart, my inspiration, and my legacy. Everything I do is for you.

Contents

Foreword

I FIRST MET Ben Utecht in 2004 when he was a senior at the University of Minnesota. I was the head coach of the Indianapolis Colts, and Ben was a tight end on the Golden Gopher football team. We were always on the lookout for talented players and Ben was very talented. But that's not what attracted my attention. We wanted more than just talented players. We wanted men who were going to be good teammates, good leaders, and people who would make a difference not just on our team, but in our city.

As a coach, I always thought the key to building championship teams was finding men of high character, bringing them together, and building on those character traits. And I could see right away Ben was just the type of young man who fit our profile. He was someone who believed in the power of culture, beliefs, and values. And once he came to the Colts he fit right in with our players. We all shared a belief that integrity, hard work, and living out your core values are essential not just in football, but in life.

Ben's story is a personal one for me because I watched him evolve both on and off the field. His dedication and commitment to excellence were evident in every practice and every game. But the beautiful thing was that Ben was not just interested in personal achievement. He wanted to help other people find success. It was that passion for helping others positively transform their lives that really stood out. Whether it was in the locker room, on the field, or in the community, Ben led by example. He was driven by the beliefs instilled in him by his family and refined during his time with the Colts.

In *The Champion's Creed*, Ben takes the principles we modeled during our Super Bowl journey and shares them in a way that transcends sports. He shows how culture is not just something that happens; it's something you create, nurture, and live out every day. I am proud of Ben for using his platform to teach others the importance of building a championship mindset in business, family, and life.

This book is filled with practical wisdom and heartfelt insight that will challenge you to rethink the way you lead and inspire those around you. I hope you'll take these lessons to heart, just as Ben did, and use them to build something truly great.

**—Tony Dungy, Hall of Fame NFL coach,
Super Bowl XLI champion, and three-time
New York Times bestselling author**

1

The Tunnel

IT WAS FEBRUARY 4, 2007. A cool mist hung in the air over the Dolphins Stadium in Miami, Florida, as Super Bowl XLI was about to begin. The weather was unusual; one of only two Super Bowls in NFL history where it rained. But the less-than-ideal conditions couldn't dampen the electric atmosphere as over 74,000 fans packed the stands, eagerly anticipating the clash between the Indianapolis Colts and the Chicago Bears.

As I stood in the concrete tunnel leading to the field, my heart was pounding. After years of sweat, sacrifice, and dedication, I had reached the pinnacle of my sport. In just moments, I would step onto the field to play in the biggest game of my life. The roar of the crowd reverberated through the tunnel, growing louder with each passing second. My teammates and I bounced on our toes, barely able to contain our excitement and nervous energy.

Finally, the signal was given. United as one, we surged forward toward the field. The tunnel attendants did their best to hold us back, fear flashing in their eyes as they faced down a stampede of wild Colts. When the gates finally opened, we exploded onto the field in a beautiful chaos of motion and sound.

Amidst the overwhelming sensory assault, one voice somehow cut through the blaring crowd. "Ben! Ben! Ben!" I was already five yards past the tunnel entrance when I heard it. Something in that voice made me slam on the brakes, even as my teammates streamed past me onto the field. I knew that voice anywhere.

Turning back toward the tunnel, I searched for its source. There, hanging halfway over the concrete railing at the mouth of the tunnel, was my father. Somehow, this small-town Minnesota minister had fought his way through the massive crowd to position himself at the exact spot where I would emerge.

As our eyes met, I saw the intense pride and love shining in his gaze. For a split second, time seemed to stand still. Here I was, moments away from playing in the Super Bowl, the culmination of my lifelong dreams. And yet my father had risked life and limb just for the chance to see me and offer a few words of encouragement before I took the field.

In that instant, I faced a choice that would come to define my life far more than anything that happened in the game itself. Part of me wanted to simply acknowledge my father with a quick wave and continue onto the field. After all, I needed to stay focused. This was the biggest moment of my career. Surely my father would understand if I didn't stop now; we could talk after the game. But as I started to turn away, I felt as if I had slammed into an invisible wall.

A quiet but powerful voice spoke in my heart: "Go back. Go back to your father. Go back to where it all began." In that moment, I was reminded of what truly mattered in life. All the fame, fortune, and accolades in the world couldn't compare to the love of family and the beliefs that had shaped me into the man I had become. Without hesitation, I spun around and sprinted back toward my father. "Dad! Dad!" I called out. Tears welled in my eyes as I reached up to clasp his outstretched hand. "I love you, Dad. It all started with you, in the backyard. Thank you for everything."

My father's eyes glistened as he replied, "I love you too, Ben. And I am so proud of you." In that powerful moment of connection,

I was transported back in time. I saw myself as a young boy, playing catch with my dad in our backyard. I remembered how he would let me tackle him, dramatically falling to the ground as if felled by my mighty strength. Those simple moments had planted the seeds of my love for football. But far more importantly, my father had used those times to instill in me the core beliefs and values that would guide me throughout my life.

His creed was simple yet profound:

- Honor God—because I believe playing for something greater than yourself produces greatness.
- Work harder than everyone else—because I believe hard work develops talent and builds character.
- Never stop improving and learning—because I believe there's always someone right behind you wanting what you have.
- Have fun—because I believe if you don't love it, what's the point?

These weren't just empty platitudes. My father lived out these beliefs and their value principles every day, leading by example. He showed me what it meant to have a strong moral compass, to persevere through adversity, to constantly strive for growth, and to approach life with joy and passion. These beliefs became the foundation upon which I built my life and career.

As I reflected on this, I realized that everyone has their own set of core beliefs instilled in them by influential figures in their lives. Whether it's a parent, grandparent, coach, teacher, or mentor, we all have those guiding principles that shape our worldview and decision-making. I wondered, what were the nonnegotiable beliefs that had most impacted my teammates' lives? What beliefs were they passing on to others?

With a renewed sense of purpose and clarity, I squeezed my father's hand one last time before jogging out onto the field.

The nerves and pressure of the moment had been replaced by a deep sense of peace and confidence. I knew who I was and what I stood for. Whatever happened in the game, I would play with honor, give maximum effort, continually adapt, and above all, enjoy every moment of this incredible experience.

As it turned out, we defeated the Chicago Bears 29-17 that night. A kid from the small river town of Hastings, Minnesota, had just played on the biggest stage in American sports, in front of over 140 million viewers worldwide. Winning the Super Bowl was a dream come true. But you know what? That brief interaction with my father before the game remains one of my most treasured memories from that night. Far more than any play on the field, that moment encapsulated everything that had brought me to that point. It reminded me of the power of love, family, and having a strong set of guiding beliefs.

My name is Ben Utecht, and my NFL Super Bowl–winning experience with Coach Tony Dungy and the Indianapolis Colts awakened my passion for helping organizations build championship cultures. You see, the lessons I learned from my father and my time in the NFL apply far beyond the football field. They are universal belief principles that can transform any team or organization. I was incredibly fortunate to play under Hall of Fame coach Tony Dungy, a man who revolutionized leadership in the NFL.

Coach Dungy's philosophy was simple but powerful: "If you build better men, you will get better football players." He understood that true success comes not just from developing skills, but from cultivating character. This approach resonated deeply with me because it aligned perfectly with the values my father had instilled. Coach Dungy didn't just pay lip service to concepts like integrity, hard work, and continuous improvement. He built his entire coaching strategy and team culture around these core beliefs. Every practice, every meeting, every interaction was infused with these principles.

The results spoke for themselves. Not only did we achieve greatness on the gridiron, but our team was known throughout the league for its strong character and positive influence both on and off the field. We weren't just great football players; we were becoming better men. As I transitioned from my playing career into the business world, I realized how rare and valuable this type of intentional culture-building truly is.

So many organizations have lofty mission statements and lists of core values plastered on their walls. But how many actually live out those ideals on a daily basis? How many have systematic approaches to reinforce and develop those values in their team members? The sad truth is that most companies' stated values are little more than empty words. They sound good in theory, but have little impact on day-to-day hiring operations or decision-making. Just look at companies like Enron, which touted "integrity" as a core value while engaging in massive fraud.

Clearly, there's often a huge gap between the values an organization claims to hold and how it actually behaves. That's why I believe it's time for a radical shift in how we approach organizational culture. We need to move beyond shallow mission statements and vague value propositions. Instead, we must develop comprehensive strategies and systems to cultivate the beliefs and behaviors we want to see in our organizations.

Think of it like creating a game plan for culture. Just as a football team meticulously prepares for each opponent, organizations need to be intentional and systematic in how they build and maintain their culture. This involves clearly defining your core beliefs, creating structures and processes to reinforce those beliefs, and holding everyone accountable to living them out.

In the pages that follow, I'll take you on a journey to transform your organizational culture. Drawing on my experiences both on and off the field, I'll provide practical insights and proven strategies for building a championship-caliber team. We'll go behind the scenes of the Super Bowl–winning Colts, examining how the culture Coach Dungy built translated into success on the field. And I'll show you how these same principles can be applied in any business or organization. You'll learn how to develop your own "Culture Creed"—a set of foundational beliefs that will guide every aspect of your organization.

The chapters will flow in and out of inspirational stories designed to connect you emotionally to the power of culture. They will also include sections focused on teaching and coaching content that will concentrate on themes and bullet-pointed practice applications designed to empower you to transform your culture through knowledge and experience.

We'll also explore how to effectively communicate these beliefs, build systems to reinforce them, and create accountability structures to ensure they're lived out at every level. The truth is, you will always have a culture in your organization—whether by design or by default. So why not be intentional about creating the culture you want? Why not build something truly extraordinary that brings out the best in every team member and drives your organization to new heights of success?

Are you ready to transform your team or organization? Are you prepared to move beyond empty platitudes and build a culture of true excellence? Then let's begin this journey together. It's time to create your championship culture.

2

What Is Culture?

ORGANIZATIONAL CULTURE IS the lifeblood of any institution, a dynamic force that shapes behavior, drives performance, and ultimately determines success. It is, as one of the foremost experts in the field, renowned organizational psychologist Dr. Edgar Schein, eloquently puts it, "a pattern of shared basic assumptions learned by a group as it solved its problems of external adaptation and internal integration."[1] This profound insight encapsulates the essence of culture as a learned phenomenon, deeply ingrained in the collective psyche of an organization.

In today's rapidly evolving business landscape, the importance of a strong, purposeful organizational culture cannot be overstated. It is the invisible hand that guides decision-making, fosters innovation, and creates a sense of belonging among team members. As leaders, we must recognize that culture is not merely a buzzword or an intangible concept, but a powerful tool that can be strategically shaped and leveraged to drive organizational success.

The foundation of a robust organizational culture lies in the alignment of beliefs, values, and behaviors. It is imperative that we, as leaders, articulate a clear set of beliefs that produce values and expectations that serve as the North Star for our teams. These objectives and aligned beliefs should be the bedrock upon

7

which we build our organizational ethos, guiding every action and decision. As John C. Maxwell, renowned leadership expert, astutely observes, "A leader is one who knows the way, goes the way, and shows the way."[2] In the context of organizational culture, this means not only defining the cultural norms but also exemplifying them in our daily conduct.

One of the most powerful aspects of organizational culture is its ability to unite diverse individuals for a common purpose. As a chief culture officer, alongside professor emeritus Dr. Daniel Zismer, I define culture as "What we believe, why we believe, and how we behave."[3] This succinct description underscores the holistic nature of culture, encompassing not just actions but also the underlying motivations and beliefs that drive them. By fostering a shared belief system, we can create a sense of unity and purpose that transcends individual differences and propels the organization toward its goals.

It is crucial to understand that organizational culture is not static; it is a living, breathing entity that requires constant nurturing and reinforcement. As leaders, we must be proactive in shaping and maintaining the desired culture. This involves not only articulating the cultural values but also embedding them in every aspect of organizational life—from hiring practices and onboarding processes to performance evaluations and reward systems. As Dr. Schein emphasizes, "The only thing of real importance that leaders do is to create and manage culture."[4]

Moreover, we must recognize that culture is not something that can be imposed from the top down. It must be inspired from top down and chosen by its members. That's how you create a culture movement. Leadership should always strive for a transformative process, not a conforming process that focuses on power and control. While leadership plays a crucial role in setting the tone, true cultural transformation occurs when every member of the organization internalizes and embodies the shared beliefs and values.

This requires consistent communication, leading by example, and creating opportunities for employees to actively participate in shaping and reinforcing the culture.

In today's increasingly complex and uncertain business environment, a strong organizational culture can be a significant source of competitive advantage. It can foster resilience, adaptability, and innovation—qualities that are essential for long-term success. As John C. Maxwell wisely states, "The pessimist complains about the wind. The optimist expects it to change. The leader adjusts the sails."[5] A robust culture equips organizations with the ability to adjust their sails in the face of changing winds, maintaining course toward their objectives.

To illustrate the power of a strong organizational culture, let's examine the case of the 2006 Indianapolis Colts, my team that achieved the pinnacle of NFL success by winning a Super Bowl championship. This triumph wasn't just a result of athletic prowess; it was a testament to the power of a carefully cultivated team culture.

The Colts' journey to success began with a deliberate choice to establish a specific cultural framework, known as the "Colts Way." This wasn't a vague concept or a catchy slogan; it was a comprehensive belief system that permeated every aspect of the organization. From the owner, Jim Irsay, down to the newest recruit, everyone was inspired to buy into and embody this culture.

At the heart of the Colts' culture was the leadership of Hall of Fame coach Tony Dungy. He recognized that a team is more than just a collection of talented individuals; it's a complex ecosystem of human beliefs, motivations, and behaviors. His challenge was to create a family out of 53 diverse individuals, each with their own backgrounds, personalities, and aspirations. We have an acronym for family in football: "Forget About Me, I Love You." Our team united through the belief that selflessness inspires commitment and loyalty.

Dungy's approach exemplifies Dr. Zismer's principle that "culture is the leader's choice."[6] He took responsibility for shaping the team's culture, making it objective and tangible rather than leaving it to chance. By drawing a clear line in the sand, Dungy created a structured environment that allowed each player to achieve their greatest potential and contribute to the team's success.

This chosen culture wasn't just about winning games; it was about fostering a sense of unity and purpose that transcended individual differences. It was about creating an environment where every team member felt valued, understood their role, and was committed to a common goal. This aligns perfectly with Dr. Schein's observation that culture is "the deeper level of basic assumptions and beliefs that are shared by members of an organization, that operate unconsciously and define in a basic 'taken for granted' fashion an organization's view of its self and its environment."[7]

The success of the Colts demonstrates that culture doesn't have to be subjective or left to chance. It can be an objective tool that directly impacts the behaviors of team members, resulting in ultimate success. This is a crucial lesson for all organizations, not just sports teams. As leaders, we have the power and responsibility to choose and shape our organizational culture deliberately.

The Colts' experience also highlights the importance of alignment between beliefs, values, and behaviors. Everything we do is connected to what we believe, and why we believe, which both drive toward how we behave. By establishing a clear set of beliefs and expectations, the Colts created a framework that guided the actions and decisions of every team member, from our star quarterback Peyton Manning to the support staff.

This alignment is crucial in any organization. When our collective behaviors are consistently guided by shared beliefs, we create a powerful synergy that can propel our organization to unprecedented heights of success and impact. It's not enough to have values written on a wall; they must be lived and breathed by every member of the organization.

The Colts' success also illustrates John C. Maxwell's observation that "The greatest leadership principle that I have ever learned in over twenty-five years of leadership is that those closest to the leader will determine the success level of that leader."[8] By cultivating a strong, positive culture, Dungy created an environment where leadership could flourish at all levels of the organization. Players felt empowered to contribute their best and to lead in their own way.

This principle applies equally in the business world. When we create a culture that empowers and inspires our team members, we multiply our leadership impact. We create an organization where everyone feels responsible for success and where leadership is not confined to those with formal titles.

The Colts' journey also demonstrates that culture is not something that can be established once and then forgotten. It requires constant reinforcement and nurturing. Dungy and his coaching staff had to consistently communicate and exemplify the cultural beliefs and values they wanted to see in the team. They had to make tough decisions that aligned with these beliefs and values, even when it might have been easier to compromise.

Now let's be honest—the NFL is an intense industry, and while I am highlighting the positive aspects of coaching behavior and intentions, we had plenty of moments where coaches and players alike failed to behave in a manner reflecting our culture. It was in those moments when we could lean on the core beliefs and values installed by Dungy's coaching style and practice a little corporate grace (okay, maybe a lot of grace sometimes), and refocus our attitudes, prioritizing a team-first mindset.

One example that comes to mind is the way in which some assistant coaches chose to motivate players to perform better. Their choice of words at times could be brutal, vulgar, and fear-based. The pressure to win blinded their ability to understand how to coach individual players in specific and intentional ways. This often resulted in a fear-based approach to performance improvement versus a value and respect strategy for development. Fear does get results but it is not sustainable and can destroy a player's confidence and joy for the game. This behavior occurs frequently in the corporate workplace as well, and should be a consistent area of focus for leadership improvement.

This consistency is crucial in any organization. Culture is not built through grand gestures or one-off initiatives; it's built through daily actions and decisions that reinforce the desired values and behaviors. As leaders, we must be vigilant in ensuring that our actions align with our stated cultural values, and we must be quick to address any deviations.

One action that accentuates behavior in alignment with a healthy culture and coaching style was Dungy's belief about how to practice being a servant leader. He was committed to finding the balance between loving a player while at the same time having to challenge them and hold them accountable to performance expectations. I was a candidate of such an action.

We were playing the Tennessee Titans and had a chance to win the game in the final minutes. A specific play we had practiced all week designed for me to score a touchdown using a mis-directional pass route was called in the huddle. As you can imagine, the pressure and excitement were intense. I couldn't wait for the ball to be snapped. "Set hut!" Peyton Manning shouted and I released. I ran through the outside shoulder of the safety and made my move, shifting toward the corner of the end zone. The ball had already been released, spiraling toward its intended target: me. Touch down, Indianapolis Colts!

I turned, hands raised in celebration, believing my catch had just won the game for our team, until I saw what looked like a beautiful yellow scarf floating through the air land close to me in the end zone. Penalty! "Offensive pass interference on number 86" declared the referee over the stadium speakers. My heart sank, and I could see the disappointment all over the faces of my teammates and coaches. Understandably I was removed from the field. Due to my mistake we scored only three points on a field goal kick, giving us a small one- or two-point lead.

Moments later, with only seconds left on the clock, the Tennessee Titans kicker launched a 62-yard bomb of a kick through the up rights to win the game. The team was devastated and I felt sick to my stomach with grief. All I could think about was what the next day's team meeting would be like.

I barely slept that night, replaying the gameday debacle over and over again, hoping that the game film would reveal that it was a poor call by the referee.

The next morning I arrived early to the practice facility to watch the film before everyone else. As I was walking down the hall toward our tight ends meeting room, Head Coach Tony Dungy came out of his office and started walking in my direction down the same hallway. My mind was racing and my thoughts telling me to turn around and head back to the locker room. In that moment, though, I felt a voice calling me to stay and trust my coach, so I did.

We both stopped to address one another, and I asked Coach Dungy if he had seen the play and what his thoughts were. He replied, "Yes, Ben, I saw the play and it was good call by the referee. You did push off of the defender to get open." My fear became a reality, but what came next was something I'll never forget—a true testament to the character of a coach who embodies servant leadership.

In Coach Dungy's *Quiet Strength* way, he preceded to prepare me for what was to come. He said something like, "Ben, this team meeting will be hard for you. You will be called out for your mistake, and it won't be easy to hear some of the corrections that are needed. But I want you to know that I believe in you and I trust that you will correct these mistakes and improve."

It was the strangest feeling. On one hand I was being prepared for something that would feel very embarrassing and uncomfortable, while on the other hand I was being empowered to believe in myself, persevere, and improve. I call this Dungy maneuver "Bold Grace."

Coach Dungy made a choice to correct me and prepare me for a difficult experience through kindness instead of anger or disappointment and also used words designed to inspire hope for the future. His strategy worked. It was a rough experience for me but I made it through and excelled going forward.

The Colts' culture was designed by a man who literally and consistently practiced what he preached and, because of that, fused 53 hardheaded individuals into one cohesive unit.

The Colts' success highlights the power of culture in uniting diverse individuals with a common purpose. In a professional sports team, as in many organizations, you have a group of individuals with diverse backgrounds, skills, and personalities. The challenge is to create a culture that respects and leverages this diversity while also creating a strong sense of unity and shared purpose.

This is increasingly important in today's globalized business environment. Organizations must create cultures that can bridge differences and create a sense of belonging for all employees, regardless of their background. The Colts' ability to create a "family" out of a diverse group of players offers valuable lessons for businesses striving to create inclusive and high-performing cultures.

Moreover, the Colts' experience demonstrates that a strong culture can be a significant source of competitive advantage. In the highly competitive world of professional sports, where talent is often evenly matched, culture can be the differentiator that leads to championship success. The same is true in business. In markets where products or services may be similar, a strong organizational culture can be the factor that attracts top talent, engages employees, satisfies customers, and ultimately drives superior performance.

The Colts' story also illustrates that culture is not just about internal dynamics; it extends to how an organization interacts with its broader community. The "Colts Way" wasn't just about winning games; it was about representing the city of Indianapolis with pride and making a positive impact off the field as well. This holistic approach to culture can inspire employees, attract fans (or customers in a business context), and build strong relationships with stakeholders.

The Colts culture was committed to be the number one community service team in the NFL. At selected times in season and each week during the offseason, players would go out into the community and provide different services like attending youth school events and programming, sport camps, speaking events, and food pantries.

Community service was a powerful component to our broader team culture. It was one of the ways in which we could practice the belief system of the "Colts Way," ultimately developing value principles in ourselves like humility and gratitude.

The journey of the Indianapolis Colts to Super Bowl champions offers powerful lessons about the importance of deliberately choosing and shaping organizational culture. It demonstrates that culture is not an intangible, uncontrollable force, but a powerful tool that leaders can and should actively manage.

As we navigate the complexities of the modern business landscape, let us take inspiration from the Colts' example. Let us recognize that we have the power to choose our organizational culture, to make it objective and actionable, and to use it as a driving force for success. Let us understand that culture is not just about what we achieve, but about who we are and how we achieve it.

As leaders, let us be those deciding the culture we want to create, and embody that culture in our actions, and show others how to live and breathe that culture every day. Let us create organizational cultures that not only drive success but also make a positive impact on our team members, our stakeholders, and the world at large.

The time is now to embrace the power of chosen culture. Whether we're leading a professional sports team or a multinational corporation, the principles remain the same. Culture can be decided, designed, deployed, and directed throughout an organization. It can be the force that unites diverse individuals, that guides behavior, that fosters innovation, and that ultimately determines success.

As we move forward, let us remember the three truths learned from the Colts' Super Bowl championship locker room:

- Culture is the human condition at work.
- Culture is the leader's choice.
- We will have a culture by design or by default, so let's go design it.

Armed with these insights, let us choose our cultures wisely, nurture them consistently, and harness their power to achieve greatness in our organizations and beyond. With that in mind, let's take a look at the intentional and nurturing insights from one of television's most impactful fictional sports culture coaches, Ted Lasso.

3

"Believe!" The Ted Lasso Effect

THE AWARD-WINNING TV show *Ted Lasso* features actor Jason Sudeikis as Coach Ted Lasso, the quirky and optimistic American football coach turned English soccer manager, having zero coaching experience in the sport. The show may seem an unlikely source of profound leadership wisdom. Yet beneath Coach Lasso's cheerful exterior and endless supply of homespun aphorisms lies a deceptively shrewd approach to building a positive team culture. By examining Ted's methods through the lens of organizational culture theory, we can extract valuable insights for leaders in any field.

"I believe in believe," Ted often declared. This simple statement encapsulates his entire philosophy on organizational culture. For Ted, cultivating belief—in oneself, in one's teammates, and in a shared vision—is the foundation of success. This aligns closely with Edgar Schein's definition of culture as "a pattern of shared beliefs, and basic assumptions."[1] Ted instinctively understands that by fostering these aligned beliefs, he can shape the behavior and performance of his team.

One of Ted's key cultural tenets is "Be a goldfish." As he explains to a discouraged player, goldfish have a 10-second memory—they quickly forget setbacks and move on. This seemingly silly advice actually embodies an important aspect of resilient organizational cultures: the ability to learn from mistakes without dwelling on them. By encouraging his team to "be a goldfish," Lasso creates an environment where players feel safe taking risks and bouncing back from failures. This fosters innovation and continuous improvement, crucial elements of adaptive cultures in today's fast-changing business landscape.

Coach Lasso's approach to leadership also exemplifies John C. Maxwell's observation that "A leader is one who knows the way, goes the way, and shows the way."[2] Despite his initial lack of soccer knowledge, Ted leads by example in embodying the cultural values he wants to instill: optimism, kindness, and continuous growth. He doesn't just preach these virtues; he lives them daily, even in the face of skepticism and ridicule. This consistency between words and actions is crucial for building trust and credibility as a cultural leader.

One of Lasso's most powerful culture-building tools is his genuine interest in every member of the organization, from star players to the kit man. He makes a point of learning everyone's names and personal details, demonstrating that every individual is valued. This approach creates a sense of belonging and personal investment in the team's success. As Dr. Daniel Zismer and I have declared, "Culture is what we believe, why we believe, and how we behave."[3] By showing genuine care for each team member, Ted shapes their beliefs about their own worth and importance to the team, which in turn influences their behavior and commitment.

I experienced the same Ted Lasso culture in the Indianapolis Colts organization. Not only did our administration and coaching staff know our names but they also supported our passions outside of football.

My rookie year in Indianapolis I was asked to speak at a large youth event in Anderson, Indiana. After my presentation, I was approached by an incredibly energetic and joyful blonde woman wearing a number 18 Peyton Manning jersey. "I'm the biggest

Colts fan you'll ever meet. No, you don't understand, I know everything about them, I just love them!"

I had the biggest smile on my face reacting to her passion as a fan. She then asked, "Can I please have your autograph?" handing me a pen and notebook. "Sure!" I exclaimed. "Who should I make it out to?" She replied, "Sandi Patty," and immediately my heart stopped beating.

I said, "Excuse me, what did you just say?"

"Sandi Patty please."

I couldn't believe it, one of the most decorated female singers in history was standing before me asking for my autograph. I immediately handed her back the pen and paper and said, "You need to sign this for me please!"

What Sandi Patty didn't realize is that my entire life was built around two equal passions, sports and music. If you've ever heard of or seen the television show *Glee*, whose main male character was the star quarterback in high school with a surprising voice, that was metaphorically me.

I was a three-sport athlete but I was also in five choirs and performed in the school musicals. My dad was a vocal music major before becoming a pastor and my mom was a talented singer as well. Growing up in the church the only voice I ever heard playing over our home speakers was Sandi Patty!

That was the start of a beautiful friendship and mentorship. While playing for the Indianapolis Colts I signed a Nashville record deal with Sandi Patty's music label and management team, along with a distribution deal from Word Entertainment. My second dream had also become a reality: to be a professional singer.

In December 2007 I was asked to take the stage with Sandi Patty and the Indianapolis Symphony Orchestra for their annual Yuletide Christmas concerts. Sandi performed every day of December, totaling over 30 concerts. I was invited to perform a special rendition of "What Are You Doing New Year's Eve?" as a duet with Sandi for as many shows as I could make. The only problem was that it was during the most important month of our NFL season. The solution? I had to muster the courage to ask our general manager, Bill Polian. and my head coach, Tony Dungy, for their blessing.

I was so nervous. My thoughts and assumptions were every-where and mostly fear-based. "What will they think of my com-mitment to the team?" "Will they doubt my focus?" "Is there going to be a consequence for even asking?"

The good news is that they already knew I could sing because even before I took the field as a player, the Colts asked me to sing the national anthem at my first ever NFL preseason football game, and I crushed it! Now that I think about it, I believe it's the only time that has ever happened in the history of the NFL.

The moment came after a long practice. I took a deep breath and pursued these two powerful leaders of the organization. I explained the amazing invitation and the time commitment needed. Just as I was expecting the rejection, they both shocked me with support.

Both Bill Polian and Tony Dungy responded with a yes, on one condition: that my focus and performance never fumbled, pun intended. My team was also supportive as both coaches and players came to one of the concerts.

It's hard to explain how much their encouragement and care for my passion and gift for singing, empowered me as a man. I developed an even stronger degree of respect and loyalty for the Colts organization. I was devoted to following through on my word by performing well on both stages, and that's what I did.

At our home win against the Jacksonville Jaguars in December 2007 I had a huge game with significant receptions. After the final seconds of the game I bolted out of the stadium, running through the downtown Indianapolis skyway system from the sta-dium to the orchestra hall, making it just in time to throw on my Colts blue tuxedo and take the stage singing a duet with multi-Grammy-winning artist Sandi Patty. It's still a pinch-myself kind of memory.

In total I performed 16 concerts with the Indianapolis Symphony Orchestra throughout that December, while playing in four NFL games as a starting tight end for the Indianapolis Colts.

Much like the fictional character of Coach Ted Lasso, Coach Tony Dungy invested in me not only as an athlete, but more importantly as a man. That kind of support motivated me to play even harder for him on every single play. The moral of this story is that great culture develops leaders who enhance the purpose behind the person, helping them to believe in their true value as a human.

Coach Lasso's "Believe" sign, which he hangs in the locker room, serves as a powerful cultural artifact. In Schein's model of organizational culture, artifacts are the visible manifestations of deeper cultural assumptions. The sign is more than just a motivational poster; it's a tangible reminder of the team's shared belief in their potential for greatness. By creating and emphasizing such cultural symbols, leaders can reinforce desired beliefs, values, and behaviors.

Another key aspect of Ted's leadership style is his emphasis on personal growth over winning at all costs. He frequently tells his players, "For me, success is not about the wins and losses. It's about helping these young fellas be the best versions of themselves on and off the field." This philosophy aligns with Tony Dungy's approach of building better men to get better football players. By prioritizing personal development, Lasso creates a culture of continuous improvement that extends beyond the soccer pitch.

Coach Lasso's handling of difficult personalities, particularly the initially antagonistic Roy Kent, demonstrates the power of a strong culture to transform individuals. Rather than trying to force Roy to conform, Ted creates an environment where Roy's natural leadership qualities can flourish in a more positive direction. This illustrates how a well-crafted culture can bring out the best in diverse individuals, uniting them with a common purpose without stifling their unique strengths.

The way Lasso navigates the transition from American football to soccer also offers lessons in cultural adaptation. Instead of trying to impose his familiar methods wholesale, Ted remains humble and open to learning. He seeks input from those with more experience in soccer, like Coach Beard and Nate the kit man. This openness to new ideas and willingness to adapt is crucial for leaders navigating cultural changes or entering new organizational contexts.

Coach Lasso's relentless positivity in the face of adversity—from skeptical fans to personal setbacks—embodies this advice from John C. Maxwell: "The pessimist complains about the wind. The optimist expects it to change. The leader adjusts the sails."[4] Ted consistently chooses to focus on opportunities rather than obstacles, a mindset that proves contagious among his team. This demonstrates how a leader's attitude can shape the overall cultural tone of an organization.

One of Lasso's most impactful cultural interventions is the "Keeley effect." By encouraging the team's fashion model marketing executive, Keeley, to humanize the players in the eyes of the fans through social media, Ted breaks down barriers between the team and the community. This strategy aligns with the idea that organizational culture extends beyond internal dynamics to how an entity interacts with its broader ecosystem. By fostering a more positive relationship with fans, Coach Lasso enhances the team's sense of purpose and connection to their community.

Lasso's approach to conflict resolution, particularly in handling the rivalry between soccer players Jamie Tartt and Roy Kent, offers valuable lessons in managing culture dynamics. Rather than taking sides or suppressing the conflict, Coach Lasso creates opportunities for the two to develop mutual understanding and respect.

This demonstrates how effective culture leadership involves not just setting rules, but facilitating experiences that allow team members to internalize cultural values.

The "Diamond Dogs"—Lasso's informal council of male colleagues—serves as an example of how subcultures can support and enrich the broader organizational culture. By creating this safe space for vulnerability and problem-solving, Ted fosters deeper bonds among key team leaders. This aligns with Schein's observation that subcultures can be a source of innovation and adaptation within larger cultural systems.

Coach Lasso's handling of the "curse" on the treatment room illustrates his respect for existing cultural beliefs while gently challenging them. Rather than dismissing the players' superstitions, he participates in the ritual to lift the curse, but does so in a way that subtly shifts the narrative toward personal responsibility and team unity. This demonstrates the delicate balance leaders must strike between honoring established culture elements and guiding culture evolution.

The way Lasso transforms the traditionally punitive "gotta get your head on straight" laps into the celebratory "Roy Kent gut-punch wind sprints" exemplifies his knack for reframing culture practices. By changing the context and meaning of the activity, Ted turns a dreaded chore into a bonding experience that reinforces team culture. This illustrates how leaders can repurpose existing cultural elements to better align with desired values and behaviors.

Lasso's creation of "Biscuits with the Boss"—his ritual of bringing homemade biscuits to team owner Rebecca Welton—demonstrates the power of personal gestures in building culture bridges. Despite Rebecca's initial hostility, Coach Lasso's persistent kindness eventually wins her over, aligning her with the team's culture direction. This shows how consistent, authentic actions can gradually shift even the most entrenched culture resistance.

The "Lasso Way" of coaching, with its emphasis on positivity, personal growth, and teamwork, bears striking similarities to the "Colts Way," described in the previous chapter. Both approaches demonstrate that a strong, intentionally crafted culture can be a powerful force for organizational success, whether in sports or in business. The key lies in clearly defining core beliefs, consistently modeling desired behaviors, and creating systems that reinforce culture values at every level of the organization.

Lasso's journey also illustrates the challenges of culture change. Despite his best efforts, Ted initially faces significant resistance from players, staff, and fans. This reflects the reality that culture transformation is often a slow, difficult process. However, Ted's persistence in the face of setbacks demonstrates the importance of long-term commitment to culture goals.

One of Coach Lasso's most powerful culture tools is his use of humor and playfulness. From his "Practice? I thought you said Pradas" joke to his endearing pop culture references, Ted uses levity to diffuse tension, build connections, and make difficult lessons more palatable. This approach creates an environment where creativity and joy are valued alongside hard work and achievement. In many traditional business settings, such playfulness might be seen as unprofessional, but Lasso's example suggests that appropriate humor can be a powerful tool for culture bonding and stress relief.

Coach Lasso's handling of star player Jamie Tartt offers insights into managing high-performing but culturally misaligned team members. Rather than immediately clashing with Jamie's ego-driven behavior, Ted seeks to understand the root causes of Jamie's attitudes and gradually guides him toward a more team-oriented mindset. This patient, developmental approach to culture alignment can be more effective than harsh enforcement of rules, particularly with valuable team members.

The contrast between Lasso's leadership style and that of his predecessor, George Cartrick, highlights the impact of culture leadership focused on team performance. Where George relied on fear and punishment, Ted fosters trust and personal growth. This shift in cultural tone translates into improved teamwork and resilience on the field. It's a powerful illustration of how culture, more than strategy or talent alone, can determine an organization's success.

Coach Lasso's approach to failure, particularly in the face of the team's relegation, offers valuable lessons in culture resilience. Rather than dwelling on the disappointment, Ted immediately refocuses the team on the opportunity for growth and redemption. This ability to maintain culture cohesion and optimism in the face of setbacks is crucial for long-term organizational success.

The way Lasso leverages the unique strengths of his coaching staff—Coach Beard's tactical knowledge, Nate's insider perspective on the players—demonstrates the power of culture inclusivity. By valuing diverse viewpoints and creating an environment where everyone feels empowered to contribute, Coach Lasso enhances the team's adaptability and innovation. This aligns with modern views on the importance of diversity and inclusion in building strong organizational cultures.

Lasso's culture leadership extends beyond the team to impact the entire Richmond community. As the team's culture improves, we see a ripple effect in fan engagement, local business support, and community pride. This illustrates how a strong organizational culture can have far-reaching positive impacts beyond the immediate confines of the organization itself.

While Coach Ted Lasso may be a fictional character, his approach to culture leadership offers very real and valuable insights for leaders in any field. By focusing on belief, personal growth, inclusivity, and persistent optimism, Ted creates a culture transformation that turns a struggling team into a cohesive, high-performing unit. His methods demonstrate that culture is indeed, as Dr. Daniel Zismer puts it, "the human condition at work,"[5] and that by intentionally shaping that condition, leaders can unlock the full potential of their organizations.

As we move forward in our exploration of organizational culture, let us carry these lessons from Coach Ted Lasso: the power of belief, the importance of valuing every team member, the transformative potential of persistent kindness, and the crucial role of leading by example. Whether we're managing a soccer team or a company, these principles can guide us in building cultures that not only drive success but also bring out the best in every individual. In Ted's words, "I believe in hope. I believe in believe." By embracing his culture strategy and applying the insights we've gleaned, we can create organizational cultures that truly believe in the potential for greatness in every team member and in the organization as a whole.

4

Culture Is the Strategy

Is PETER DRUCKER'S famous quote "Culture eats strategy for breakfast" true or false? I say false! I believe Peter missed the mark because his statement seems to separate culture from strategy. I believe they are one and the same. Culture should be the primary strategy of every organization that drives and applies all sub-strategies and operational systems that make businesses successful. I believe if culture is the strategy, then it will eat every meal at every time of the day!

First, the culture strategy has to be well defined. It needs to be a transcendent belief that takes all members of an organization to achieve. In the case of my team, the Indianapolis Colts, the highest belief was that we would win a Super Bowl, but it would demand a championship level of practiced behavior from everyone.

It reminds me of a famous story about a janitor at NASA. President John F. Kennedy was touring the NASA campus when he came across a janitor working diligently to clean the hallways of the NASA facilities.

The president stopped to introduce himself to the janitor and asked one question of the committed employee. "Sir, what's your job here at NASA?" Without missing a beat the janitor responded, "Mr. President, my job is to put a man on the moon!"

Now, we could just cast that aside as a small inspirational anecdote, or maybe a momentary example of having a good workplace attitude. Or we could consider that the overarching culture belief strategy was that every member of the NASA team—whether an astronaut or a facilities manager—was inspired, trained, and unified by the same purpose of belief. We all play a role in putting a human being on the moon.

It was no different in Indianapolis with the Colts. Coach Dungy believed in the same strategy, and he communicated that clearly to the entire organization. He wanted all members of the Colts organization to be aligned on the belief that every single one of them was a significant piece in this Super Bowl–sized puzzle.

From owner Jim Irsay to the coaching staff and players, training and equipment staff, facilities management, and all business administration, every single person who worked for this organization was connected by a singular culture strategy belief: "We believe our job is to win a Super Bowl!" The evidence for the equity of that shared belief strategy was that the entire organization, all of its people, received a World Championship Super Bowl ring.

For an organization, when you lead by inspiring all members to believe in the same culture strategy, there is nothing that you cannot achieve.

The intertwining of culture and strategy is a concept that has gained significant traction in organizational psychology and management literature. As Dr. Edgar Schein states, "Culture and leadership are two sides of the same coin."[1] This perspective emphasizes the inseparable nature of culture and strategy in organizational success.

To understand why culture must be the strategy of an organization, we need to examine the fundamental nature of both concepts. Strategy relates to positioning and advancing the organization's mission. Culture, on the other hand, encompasses the beliefs, values, and behaviors that shape the organization's identity and guide its actions.

Dr. Cameron and Dr. Quinn, in their book *Diagnosing and Changing Organizational Culture*, argue that "organizational culture is not just a powerful factor in organizations; it is the prime competitive advantage when it is aligned with strategy and leadership."[2] This alignment is crucial for translating strategy into action and achieving organizational goals. In other words, culture must be the strategy.

Let's explore how five NFL culture strategies from my Indianapolis Colts experience can be applied to business contexts.

No Excuses! No Explanations!"

I'll never forget seeing this phrase in big blue letters on the white wall as I entered our locker room for the first time. I knew this team strived for perfection, and believed they would be World Champions. I also learned that there is an ending to that quote: "The only way to win is by execution!"

We believed, supported by *Pro Football Reference: Turnover Data*, that most losses came from teams who made the most mistakes. This provided us with the goal of being the most prepared and practiced team in the NFL.

When we stepped onto the field for gameday there would be total confidence regarding what our job was on that day and how well we understood the strategy for our opponent. We believed that expectation held us accountable to have "no excuses or explanations" for mistakes we made due to mental error from not being well prepared. The results were highly successful.

"Winning" was defined on multiple levels within individual position, offense, defense, special teams, collective team, and organization.

All of these subcultures within the organization aligned on what "winning" meant under the all-encompassing culture of the organization. The main belief held by every individual in the Colts organization—from owner Jim Irsay to every athlete, training staff, facilities management, business administration, and so on—was "We are here to win a Super Bowl and become World Champions."

In business, this principle translates to a culture of accountability and ownership. For example:

- A software development company implementing a "blameless post-mortem" process after project failures, focusing on learning and improvement rather than finger-pointing
- A retail chain establishing clear performance metrics for each store and holding regular review meetings to address shortfalls and celebrate successes

Strategy as the Key to Success on the Field

There were four champion pillars in place that I believe enabled us to practice a winning strategy. One of those principles was seen through the lens of being a champion learner. Learning was an essential component to winning because we competed against a new opponent every week. This meant the game strategy was completely different every seven days. In order to be successful we practiced a system built around questions, execution, and evaluation. These three facets were critical strategic factors in being the most prepared team on the NFL field.

In the business world, this principle emphasizes the importance of strategic planning and execution. Examples include:

- A startup conducting regular market research and pivoting its product offerings based on customer feedback and emerging trends

- A manufacturing company investing in predictive mainte-nance technology to minimize downtime and improve operational efficiency

There Are No Foolish Questions

In Indianapolis we lived in an ecosystem of seeking continuous clarity through healthy questioning. The belief was that ques-tions resulted in complete clarity of expectation, which improved performance greatly. We were called upon to ask questions in every meeting and during every practice because we couldn't afford to ask questions on gameday. The goal was zero insecurity about asking questions, and that environment empowered us to reach our potential as mental and physical athletes.

A culture of curiosity and continuous learning is crucial in business. This can be applied through:

- Implementing regular "Ask Me Anything" sessions with leadership to encourage open communication and transparency
- Creating cross-functional teams to tackle complex prob-lems, leveraging diverse perspectives and expertise

Execution

This was the opportunity for us to put the answers we received from asking questions to the test. Our practices were built around a specific number of repetitions. The average NFL offense on gameday runs about 60–65 plays. Coach Dungy made sure we practiced between 90 and 100 during our heaviest practices of the week. This strategy of replicating execution prepared us in every possible way to react to the constant changes and adaptations that would come from our opponents. Practice is the key to a sustainable culture of "strategy" designed for "winning."

In business, execution is about turning plans into action. Examples include:

- A marketing team running AB tests on multiple campaign variations to optimize performance before a full-scale launch
- A logistics company simulating various supply chain disruptions to prepare contingency plans and improve resilience

Evaluation

Every minute of every single practice was videotaped, which provided a level of accountability that surpasses most industry capabilities today. I called this belief system "The eye in the sky doesn't lie." The foundational strategy behind evaluation was *accountability*. We practiced this by reviewing every single minute of practice and game film. This allowed us to see all of our own growth areas and focus on how to improve them, along with providing an opportunity to study the weaknesses of our opponents that we could take advantage of. Practicing a belief system around elite accountability will greatly improve individual and team growth opportunities, providing high-level performance, which improves the bottom line. What is the bottom line? "Winning!"

Continuous evaluation and improvement are essential for business success. This can be implemented through:

- Implementing a robust performance management system that includes regular feedback and development plans
- Conducting thorough post-project reviews to identify lessons learned and areas for improvement in future initiatives

Dr. John Kotter, a leading expert on change management, emphasizes the importance of aligning culture with strategy: "Culture is not something you 'fix.' Rather, you shape it with your actions and behaviors."[3] This perspective underscores the need for leaders to actively cultivate a culture that supports and drives the organization's strategy.

Moreover, research by Daniel R. Denison, who is widely recognized for his research on the link between organizational culture and performance, and Aneil K. Mishra, who focuses on the impact of organizational trust and culture on organizational performance, has shown that organizations with strong, strategically aligned cultures significantly outperform their peers in terms of profitability, growth, and market value. In their 1995 study, Denison and Mishra state, "Organizations with participative cultures and those with an emphasis on adaptability and mission are more likely to achieve superior business performance."[4]

This further reinforces the notion that culture must be the strategy for long-term success. As Denison and Mishra espouse from the same study, "Our research indicates that organizations that emphasize a strong sense of mission and consistent values are likely to perform better over time."[5]

The concept of culture as strategy also addresses the challenge of strategy implementation. As noted by Bains & Company, 65% of organizations struggle with poor execution.[6] By making culture the strategy, organizations can create a shared sense of purpose and direction that guides decision-making at all levels, improving the likelihood of successful strategy execution.

The idea that culture must be the strategy of an organization is supported by both academic research and practical experience. By aligning beliefs, values, and behaviors with strategic objectives, organizations can create a powerful competitive advantage that drives success across all aspects of the business. A Peter Drucker insight I agree with says, "The best way to predict the future is to create it." By making culture the strategy, organizations are not just predicting their future—they're actively shaping it.

To fully embrace this concept, organizations should consider the following steps:

1. Clearly define and communicate the organization's beliefs and values.
2. Align hiring practices with cultural fit as well as technical skills.
3. Develop leadership training programs that emphasize cultural stewardship.
4. Implement recognition and reward systems that reinforce desired behaviors and outcomes.
5. Regularly assess and refine the organization's culture to ensure it remains aligned with strategic goals. By taking these actions, organizations can create a culture that not only supports their strategy but becomes their strategy, driving success and sustainability in an ever-changing business landscape.

The core to every successful strategy in life and business begins with your foundational beliefs. Defining, understanding, and practicing those beliefs will ultimately breathe life into your value principles. Every organization and its leaders should consider the culture position that beliefs drive company values into significance and action.

5

Beliefs Drive Values

At the heart of every great organization lies a set of core beliefs that shape its identity, guide its actions, and define its culture. These chosen beliefs are the bedrock upon which the value principles of an organization are built, creating a powerful framework that drives success and inspires greatness. In this chapter, I will highlight specific themes and explore the profound impact of objective chosen beliefs on organizational culture, drawing insights from literature, expert opinions, and historical examples.

The Foundation of Organizational Culture: Chosen Beliefs and Value Principles

One of the core beliefs of Coach Dungy's Colts culture strategy was "Family Saturdays." Saturday practices in the NFL were light and restorative in nature. They were designed to put the finishing touches on the upcoming game's strategy.

As athletes we would dress in our Colts performance sweat suits and take the field for an hour walk-jog performance-level practice. What made our Saturdays unique was the family application. Coach Dungy invited players with families, wives, and children to come and be a part of that Saturday home game practice.

Imagine being the child of one of these elite athletes and getting the opportunity to come and watch your dad in an NFL practice. What an exciting and uplifting opportunity! But some of the players without kids and with a high level of focus and an elite attitude for preparation might have a different story to tell, and that included our All-Pro quarterback Peyton Manning.

As the story goes, Peyton was frustrated that during one Saturday practice he couldn't focus and throw a pass to one of our star receivers because his young son was hanging all over his dad on the field. Peyton made sure to have a correctional conversation with Coach Dungy about the merits of "Family Saturdays."

One can totally understand the reaction to a standardized situation that at times can make preparation difficult, but it never changed while I was there. Coach Dungy's belief communicated the importance of pouring into something that was bigger than a game: family.

Years later after Coach Dungy retired and became a part of the sports entertainment community as a TV NFL sports anchor, he was working at a home game for the Denver Broncos. This was the team that Peyton Manning had just transferred to over the course of the offseason. In many ways it was a perfect reunion between head coach and star quarterback.

Before the game, one of our former star receivers with the Colts, Brandon Stokely, ran over to Coach Dungy on the sidelines. He preceded to share with Dungy surprising news that Coach might not believe. During the first week of practice with the Denver Broncos, Peyton Manning announced in a team meeting that the team would be installing "Family Saturdays" as a part of their team culture.

After the game, Coach Dungy described his elation when watching his former quarterback stand at the press conference podium while both of his young children clung to his legs with uncertain excitement. Imagine the pride in watching a human you coached develop into a leader who placed family above all else.

Identifying what you believe, why you believe it, and how you hope it will be embodied provides significant clarity growth and accountability. That is why developing your culture creed is a foundational strategy in building workplace environments that focus on positively impacting people first.

Now let's focus on the transformative power of creeds in shaping behavior and fostering commitment within communities. Finally, we will set the stage for an exciting exploration of how these principles were applied in the realm of professional football to develop a winning culture.

The Greatest Franchise CEO in History

Scott Hillstrom, a trusted friend and brilliant business lawyer and winner of the International Franchise of the Year award from the International Franchise Association, shared a remarkable story that illustrates this point. After receiving the award, Hillstrom was invited to a table with some of the greatest franchise minds in the world. A question was posed: "Who is the greatest franchise CEO in history?" To Hillstrom's surprise, every single franchise leader at the table unanimously answered, "Jesus!"

The reasoning behind this unexpected answer is profound. These business leaders recognized that Jesus took an objective belief system, taught it to 12 men, developed them, inspired them to practice it, and then commissioned them to replicate it. Today, over 2.6 billion people around the world identify Christianity as their personal belief.

Regardless of one's feelings toward religion, this stands as the most compelling evidence of a scalable belief system the world has ever seen—and it continues to grow. Dr. Ken Blanchard, a renowned leadership expert and author, supports this view in his book *Lead Like Jesus*, stating, "Jesus is the greatest leadership model of all time."[1] Blanchard argues that Jesus's leadership was rooted in a clear set of beliefs and values, which he not only taught but also lived out in his daily life. This consistency between belief and action created a powerful example that inspired his followers and continues to influence people today.

The transformative power of Jesus's leadership is evident in the rapid spread and enduring impact of Christianity. As noted by historian Rodney Stark in his book *The Rise of Christianity*, "The mission of the church was to change the world, not to retreat from it."[2] This mission, driven by core beliefs and values, led to the formation of one of the largest and most influential movements in human history.

The Power of Chosen Beliefs in Organizational Culture

Dr. Tony Bridwell, a renowned expert in organizational culture and leadership—but more importantly my dear friend and mentor—emphasizes the critical role of beliefs in shaping corporate culture. In his book *The Kingmaker: A Leadership Story of Integrity and Purpose*, Bridwell writes, "Culture is not something you can simply mandate or declare. It is the result of shared beliefs, values, and behaviors that are reinforced over time."[3] This insight underscores the importance of clearly defining and articulating the foundational beliefs that will guide an organization's culture.

Bridwell further elaborates on the connection between beliefs and values, stating, "Values are the outward expression of our inward beliefs. When we align our beliefs with our values, we create a powerful force that drives behavior and shapes culture."[4] This alignment is crucial for creating a cohesive and authentic organizational culture that resonates with employees and stakeholders alike.

The Role of Creeds in Shaping Community Behavior

Throughout history, creeds have played a crucial role in guiding the behaviors and commitments of different communities. A creed, defined as "a set of beliefs that guides the behaviors of a person or group," serves as a powerful tool for articulating and reinforcing shared beliefs and values. One of the most well-known examples of a creed shaping community behavior is the Nicene Creed, formulated in AD 325. This creed unified Christian beliefs and has been recited by millions of Christians for centuries, reinforcing their shared faith and guiding their actions.

Similarly, the United States Constitution and its Preamble serve as a kind of national creed, outlining the fundamental beliefs and values that shape American society and governance.

There is also historical evidence of "pirate creeds" or "pirate codes" stemming from various sources, most notably the "Articles of Agreement" or "Pirate Codes" established across many pirate crews during the Golden Age of Piracy (circa 1650–1730). These creeds functioned as a comprehensive set of beliefs and rules governing crew behavior, and while they varied between ships, they often addressed similar themes.

These creeds played a crucial role in maintaining order and discipline among pirate crews, who endured cramped living conditions and faced constant peril. The creeds embodied a blend of pragmatism and mutual respect, ensuring equitable treatment for all crew members within the context of their piratical society. They covered aspects such as the distribution of plunder, compensation for injuries, and punishments for infractions.

While the concept of a pirate's creed seems only theatrical in our movies, it was rooted in practical, nonnegotiable beliefs and rules that were essential for maintaining crew morale, survival, and success in the dangerous world of piracy.

Dr. Bridwell emphasizes the importance of such creeds in his work on organizational culture. He states, "A well-crafted creed can serve as a north star for an organization, providing clarity and guidance in times of uncertainty and change."[5] This underscores the potential of creeds to shape and maintain a strong organizational culture.

I recently had the privilege of meeting and befriending an exceptional business leader from the United Kingdom, a gentlemen by the name of Mark Markiewicz. Mark shared a powerful story about an article he wrote called "Business as Mission," or "How two grocers changed the course of a Nation." Mark began to teach me about the history of registered businesses in the United Kingdom and that every formed company had been accounted for since the beginning of their corporate registry.

One of the first companies formed was called the Most Worshipful Company of Mercantilists or "Grocers." The company's history dates back to the early 1800s and transformed the business culture of the nation because of its intense focus on articulating and applying Christian belief principles to business behaviors.

It ultimately became an association of companies all deeply committed to practicing a creed that outlined essential beliefs and values that must be practiced. In order to join the association, you had to pledge your allegiance to its purpose.

The mercantilists' dedication resulted in the production of a profound work of literature called "Some Rules for the Conduct of Life." It highlighted 36 individual and highly impactful beliefs that were designed to inspire and govern human behavior.

To this day that association still exists and thrives, not only to perform at a high level in business but, more importantly, to positively influence all who come in contact with their brands.

Developing a Healthy Culture: Insights from Dr. Tony Bridwell

I want to take a moment to spotlight the importance of creating a mentorship culture. I met Dr. Tony Bridwell two years ago as I was beginning to build my career around organizational culture. I needed guidance and education.

It is amazing how God has used multiple Tonys in my life to promote growth. Tony Bridwell not only listened well during our first meeting but responded with an invitation to build a deep and meaningful relationship with him designed to develop my gifts and talents toward the goal of helping companies excel in their culture dreams.

I meet with Dr. Bridwell consistently, in order to learn the nuances of culture development. Tony's expertise as the chief people officer at multiple Fortune 100 companies and a significant author has been radically transformational for my life.

His extensive work on organizational culture provides valuable insights into the process of developing a healthy and high-performing culture. Insight from his book *The Kingmaker* emphasizes the importance of aligning personal and organizational values: "When individuals find alignment between their personal values and the values of their organization, they become fully engaged and committed to the mission."[6]

In his writing, he also stresses the role of leadership in cultivating a positive culture: "Leaders must be intentional about creating a culture that brings out the best in people. This requires a clear understanding of the organization's beliefs and values, and a commitment to living them out every day." This perspective highlights the critical connection between chosen beliefs, leadership behavior, and organizational culture.

Dr. Tony Bridwell outlines a framework for developing a healthy culture:

1. Clarify core beliefs and values.
2. Communicate these beliefs and values consistently.
3. Align systems and processes with the desired culture.
4. Model the desired behaviors at all levels of leadership.
5. Recognize and reward behaviors that reinforce the culture.

This framework provides a practical approach to translating chosen beliefs into a tangible and sustainable organizational culture.

The Culture Creed: A Tool for Organizational Transformation

Recognizing the power of creeds in shaping behavior and culture, the concept of a "Culture Creed" emerges as a powerful tool for organizational transformation. A Culture Creed serves as an inspirational and educational onboarding and development manual that enhances an organization's ability to penetrate the minds and hearts of every team member, improving their knowledge and application of the behaviors expected to reflect the exclusive beliefs and value strategy of the organization.

The key to developing an effective organizational creed lies in articulating:

- What you believe about your values
- Why you believe in your values
- How you believe your values should be manifested in workplace behavior

By creating and implementing a Culture Creed, organizations can go beyond traditional mission and value statements to create a living document that guides behavior, decision-making, and overall organizational culture. This creed becomes a powerful marketing and talent acquisition tool, setting the organization apart from its competition and attracting individuals who align with its core beliefs and values. I will dive deeper into the Culture Creed in Chapter 8.

The NFL Experience: A Creed-Driven Winning Culture

As we conclude this exploration of the power of chosen beliefs in shaping organizational culture, we stand on the brink of an exciting revelation. How can the principles we've discussed be applied in the high-stakes, high-performance world of professional sports? More specifically, how did a creed play a role in developing a winning culture within an NFL team?

The story of how a carefully crafted creed transformed the culture of a professional football team is a testament to the power of shared beliefs and values. It demonstrates how even in the most competitive and pressure-filled environments, a strong culture foundation can drive success and create lasting impact.

The journey from chosen beliefs to a thriving organizational culture is one of intentionality, consistency, and unwavering commitment. As we prepare to explore the NFL experience in greater detail, consider the potential implications for your own organization. How might a well-defined set of beliefs, articulated through a powerful creed, transform your corporate culture? What could be achieved if every member of your team was united by a shared set of values and commitments?

The lessons I learned from within the Indianapolis Colts Super Bowl Championship NFL locker room, led by Hall of Fame General Manager Bill Polian and Hall of Fame Head Coach and servant leadership expert Tony Dungy, have the potential to revolutionize the way you approach culture-building in your own organization. This experience, born out of a passion for developing high-performing cultures, offers invaluable insights into the practical application of the principles we've discussed.

As we delve deeper into this inspiring case study in the next chapter, prepare to be inspired by the transformative power of a culture built on a foundation of shared beliefs and values. The story of how the Indianapolis Colts practiced a creed to achieve greatness not only in football but in building a cohesive and high-performing team culture will provide concrete examples and actionable insights that you can apply to your own organization.

By understanding and implementing the principles of belief-driven culture, articulated through a powerful creed, you can create an organizational environment that not only achieves remarkable results but also fosters personal growth, commitment, and fulfillment among your team members. The journey ahead promises to be both enlightening and transformative, offering an opportunity to produce a sustainable culture movement across an organization through the power of shared beliefs and values.

6

The Culture Movement

I HAVE ACTUALLY played a role in the start of a culture movement. What makes a movement meaningful? It's because it originates out of an individual or group nonnegotiable belief that turns into action.

In August 2008, my NFL football career came to an abrupt end. During the Cincinnati Bengals training camp I unfortunately experienced my fifth diagnosed concussion.

I was unconscious on the field for over a minute and remember regaining consciousness as I was being strapped to a gurney and rushed to the hospital. It all happened on national television as HBO's *Hardknocks* was chronicling our team and upcoming season.

In the blink of an eye my entire NFL football dream was over. My dad always told me, "Where one door closes, another door will open, so keep your head up and watch."

That door did open, into a room I didn't expect: the world of neurology. Shortly after I retired I was pursued to write a book about my life and concussion story called *Counting the Days While My Mind Slips Away: A Story of Perseverance and Hope*.

The title was actually the first line in a song I wrote for my wife and daughters as a love letter in case I had to face the trepidation of future brain disease. The song is called "You Will Always Be My Girls."

The door opened into a world of philanthropy for brain health was unexpected. The NFL Players Association (NFLPA) asked me to testify in a congressional hearing in Washington, DC. The theme was traumatic brain injury in sports and its future consequences on player health.

In that hearing I shared my concussion story for the first time. I had to relive multiple injuries and be vulnerable about the love letter I wrote to my wife and four daughters about my fears for an uncertain future. A month before this hearing I co-authored and produced a music video for the song I wrote for my family, but wisdom deep within told me to wait on releasing it, so I paused.

After the congressional hearing, the media was fascinated over hearing this song and experiencing the music video. I knew the time was now. I launched the music video on that day, and within 48 hours it was already heading toward a million views.

Shortly after that congressional experience I was awarded the Public Leadership In Neurology Award (PLINA) by the American Academy of Neurology (AAN), the most prestigious neurology association in the world. Remarkably, the AAN headquarters is in my home state of Minnesota. In conjunction with accepting the award I was asked to be AAN's national spokesperson on concussion. I executed that role for two years and then transitioned to their public board at the American Brain Foundation.

During this season of life, I entered into an arbitration process with the Cincinnati Bengals organization over the details on how I was released from the team before being medically cleared healthy by my physicians. It turned out to be the longest grievance in NFL history because of its focus on concussions.

After three years of waiting, my legal representation at the NFLPA notified me of our success in winning the grievance hearing. This was financially significant for our family, but equally important, it set precedent for how future players would be treated for a concussion injury and set the groundwork for new return-to-play concussion protocols.

The production of Will Smith's movie *Concussion*, along with the NFLPA's dedication to player health and safety, and my national advocacy participation with the AAN, initiated a focal movement on the essential importance of athlete brain health. Today the NFL and NCAA follow strict guidelines regarding concussion practices, and all 50 states in America now have concussion legislation.

This was a movement born out of the belief that your brain is the most vital element in your body. Your brain is what makes you human. Your brain is your soul. My advocacy movement message was a "Pro Brain, Pro Game" campaign. We can celebrate and care for both at the same time.

Organizations can and do make an impact through movements that reflect their core beliefs. By doing so, they have redefined their industries and what is expected of them.

In the aftermath of the 2008 housing and mortgage industry crash, an unlikely champion emerged from the world of professional sports. Casey Crawford, a former Super Bowl–winning tight end for the Tampa Bay Buccaneers, decided to tackle a new challenge in the mortgage industry. Standing at an impressive 6 feet 6 inches, Crawford was not only a giant on the football field but would soon become a colossus in transforming the toxic and broken landscape of mortgage lending. His weapon of choice? A culture movement.

It's fitting that Crawford named his company "Movement Mortgage." In the 16 years since the financial crisis, he and his team built one of the largest, most successful, and, more importantly, most impactful mortgage companies in the United States. Movement Mortgage told a story unprecedented in the industry— one that focused on how well they served their internal team members and every person who chose them to help achieve their American Dream.

The company's revolutionary message was simple yet powerful: "Love God, and Love People" above all else. This ethos sent shockwaves through the industry, with Crawford becoming the champion for this cause. His story has taken him across the country, appearing on major media platforms to redefine how an essential product can be delivered in a way that focuses on transforming the human condition of everyone who comes in contact with their brand.

Movement Mortgage disrupted the industry by prioritizing culture, community impact, and philanthropy over mere profit. Their model centers on providing excellent customer service while reinvesting in underserved communities, creating a ripple effect of positive social impact. Their tagline, "A Movement of Change," perfectly encapsulates their beliefs and actions.

The company's organizational culture strategy is built on four foundational mission platforms that set them apart in the marketplace:

- **Culture:** Deeply rooted in the mission to love and value people, Movement Mortgage fosters an employee-centric environment promoting purpose, teamwork, and service. Employees are encouraged to give back through volunteerism and community engagement, which is woven into daily operations.
- **Impact lending:** This initiative partners with developers and nonprofits to create affordable housing and foster sustainable community projects. They offer financing solutions specifically designed to benefit underserved communities, facilitating both homeownership and revitalization efforts.
- **Movement foundation:** As the philanthropic arm of the company, the Movement Foundation reinvests profits into various community-centered initiatives. Their work spans affordable housing, healthcare clinics, and community services, aimed at addressing systemic inequities.
- **Movement schools:** This network of public charter schools offers high-quality education in low-income neighborhoods.

The schools focus on personalized learning, fostering a culture of care, and holistic development for each student.

How does any movement begin? It starts with an individual or group recognizing a need for change. Based on their intrinsic beliefs about the desired need, a deep level of commitment and devotion to the cause or mission is born, and the movement begins.

Michael Brennan, the former president of Movement Mortgage and industry expert, said, "Movements culture is defined by our intentionality around taking action. It starts and ends with our mission statement, to love and value people in everything we do; it is our DNA!"[1]

Leading with the organizational belief that love can transform people sets Movement Mortgage apart from the rest of the competition. Their approach to loving people is what inspires their team members to choose to believe in their culture. When a community is aligned on a belief, you create an opportunity to launch a culture movement.

Kent Myers—CEO, PhD in leadership, and culture expert— emphasizes that "in order for culture to scale across an organization and become sustainable, it must originate out of a movement and not a program." Programs can demand conformity and obedience without inspiration, whereas a movement begins through aligned belief and transformation. Company team members must first believe in the culture beliefs and values being espoused to be inspired to practice them. However, these beliefs and values can't be practiced without a culture strategy and system in place that supports the ability to develop organizational values in people.

To create a culture movement, one must identify the foundational beliefs that inspire values and then hire toward those nonnegotiable beliefs and values. This process ensures stronger success in creating higher degrees of culture alignment across an organization.

Culture: The Feeling Is "Mutual"

One Fortune 100 company I have worked with in Minnesota that is exemplifying this approach is Northwestern Mutual, named by *Fortune* as "one of the world's most admired life insurance" companies. With an estimated six thousand to seven thousand employees, they are known for their intentional efforts to produce a healthy and high-performing culture.

What stands out about Northwestern Mutual's organizational culture strategy is that it leads with beliefs. Rarely do companies choose to identify core beliefs over core values, but Northwestern Mutual does, and their internal, client, and community impact is evident across the country. Let's explore the essential beliefs of Northwestern Mutual:

- **"We believe in putting people first.** As a mutual company, people are our DNA. We don't have shareholders, so instead of reporting to Wall Street, we give our policyowners governance rights. And since our company belongs to them, our profits go to them in the form of dividends."
- **"We believe in the expertise of our financial advisors.** Your financial go-to. Your trusted partner who helps you continue to reach goal after goal. These expert listeners hear what's most important to you and put the right financial options and strategies into a personalized plan designed to make it happen. All in a pressure-free, judgment-free environment."
- **"We believe in being our best, even when things look their worst.** The year was 1859. An ox and a passenger train collided just outside Johnson Creek, Wisconsin, and two of our policy owners lost their lives in the wreck. The claims totaled $3,500, which was $1,500 more than our two-year-old company had on hand. Our then-president, Samuel S. Daggett, and his fellow trustees personally

borrowed the money to settle the claims, proving that our dedication to our clients has been around as long as the company itself."

- **"We believe in inclusion.** We know that the collective ideas, opinions, and creativity of a diverse workforce is necessary to deliver the innovative financial solutions our clients need. It's why we're committed to creating a singular culture of inclusion and respect."
- **"We believe in our communities.** Where we live and the communities we build are at the core of who we are. That's why we believe in giving back. Together with our partners we're improving education, revitalizing neighborhoods, and accelerating the search for better treatments and cures for childhood cancer."
- **"We believe in leading by example.** From our CEO to our Board of Trustees, our leaders live and breathe the principles Northwestern Mutual was founded on, doing what's right for our clients, taking the long view, delivering superior product value, building lifelong relationships, and maintaining exceptional financial strength. And they inspire the rest of our employees and advisors to do the same."[2]

It is refreshing to see a company as successful as Northwestern Mutual leading their culture and services through the power of belief.

Mahatma Gandhi said, "Be the change that you wish to see in the world." Change only comes through action, and action is a byproduct of belief. Movement Mortgage and Northwestern Mutual are two champion examples of organizations that have designed their culture around their beliefs, creating a culture movement that is providing significant impact on the human condition in business and in life.

These companies demonstrate that a strong organizational culture rooted in core beliefs can drive success while making a positive impact on employees, customers, and communities. By prioritizing beliefs and values over mere profit, they've shown that it's possible to create thriving businesses that also contribute meaningfully to society. As more companies adopt this approach, we may see a shift in how businesses operate and interact with the world around them, potentially leading to more sustainable and socially responsible practices across various industries.

My experience on an NFL Super Bowl championship team taught me that every organization can create a blueprint for culture success. Let me bring you onto the sideline and into the huddle of the Indianapolis Colts culture.

7

Blueprint of a Super Bowl Culture

THE GAME PLAN for building a championship culture in Indianapolis focused on a handful of profound themes that I will spotlight throughout this chapter. As you read, consider how you might build your own culture playbook for your life or business.

The Foundations of Championship Culture: Lessons from the NFL

When I first stepped into an NFL team meeting room as a rookie, I was awestruck. Sitting around me were some of the greatest players in the league—future Hall of Famers like Peyton Manning, Marvin Harrison, Dwight Freeney, and Edgerrin James. But it wasn't their athletic prowess that left the most lasting impression. It was the words of our Hall of Fame head coach, Tony Dungy, that truly transformed my perspective on what it meant to be successful, both on and off the field.

Dungy began by quoting his former Pittsburg Steeler coach, Chuck Noll: "Men, if you're sitting in this room and your entire identity is wrapped up in a sport, you've totally missed the purpose of your life." Those words hit me like a ton of bricks. All my life,

I had put football at the center of my identity, believing it was the key to success. Yet here was my new coach telling me that my purpose extended far beyond the playing field—that my value as a human being transcended my athletic abilities. This moment marked the beginning of a profound shift in my understanding of success, leadership, and personal growth.

Over my years with the Indianapolis Colts, I witnessed and participated in the development of a championship culture built on foundational beliefs and values that went far beyond Xs and Os and straight into the minds and hearts of the players. The goal was to improve as men.

As Tony Dungy writes in his book *Quiet Strength*, "I've said many times that the secret to success is good leadership, and the secret to good leadership is all about making the lives of your team members or workers better."[1] This philosophy permeated every aspect of our organization, from how we practiced to how we interacted with each other and the community. It was a culture that emphasized personal growth, mutual respect, and unwavering commitment to shared values.

In the years since my retirement from the NFL, I've reflected deeply on what made the Colts' culture so special and effective. Through this process of discovery, I've identified four foundational principles that I believe were key to our success—what I call the "Four Ls": Listening, Learning, Language, and Love. When practiced consistently and intentionally, these principles have the power to transform not just sports teams, but any organization or individual seeking to achieve greatness.

Let's explore each of these principles in depth, examining how they were implemented in the Colts' organization and considering how they can be applied in various aspects of life and business. By the end, I hope you'll have a new perspective on what it truly means to build a championship culture—one that values personal growth, mutual respect, and the pursuit of excellence in all areas of life.

Listening: The Foundation of Successful Communication

At the heart of any successful team or organization is effective communication, and at the core of effective communication is the ability to listen. Listening requires a selfless attitude. It reminds me of something Coach Dungy espoused: You can accomplish anything if you stop caring about who gets the credit.

In the fast-paced, high-pressure world of professional football, you might think that listening would take a back seat to more active, assertive forms of communication. But in the Colts' organization, we understood that being a champion listener was just as crucial as being a champion athlete.

The importance of listening was exemplified in one of the most fundamental aspects of football: the huddle. While it might seem mundane to outside observers, we recognized the huddle as the foundation of our offense. It was in these brief moments, repeated 65–75 times per game, that information vital to our success was communicated. Our offensive coordinator, Tom Moore, instilled in us a "culture of the huddle" built on three key principles: Stop, Look, and Care.

1. **Stop:** This was an act of selflessness. The moment our quarterback, Peyton Manning, stepped into the huddle, we were expected to cease all other thoughts and give him our full attention. This practice taught us the value of being present and focused in the moment.

2. **Look:** This represented the pursuit of information. We were instructed not just to listen to Peyton, but to look directly at his mouth as he spoke. In a stadium filled with 80,000 screaming fans, visual cues could be just as important as auditory ones. This practice emphasized the importance of using all available means to gather information.

3. **Care:** This was the practice of empathy. We were expected to put ourselves in the shoes of each of our teammates, understanding that their roles and responsibilities directly impacted our own. This fostered a sense of interconnectedness and mutual responsibility.

These principles extended far beyond the huddle. They became a framework for how we approached all communication within our organization. By practicing these skills consistently, we became not just better football players, but better communicators and team members. As Tony Dungy writes in *Uncommon*: "Listening is an art that requires attention over talent, spirit over ego, others over self."[2]

Reflective Questions:

1. In your personal and professional life, how often do you practice truly stopping to give others your full attention when they speak?
2. How can you incorporate multiple senses (like both listening and watching) to improve your information gathering in various situations?
3. How might practicing empathy and care in your listening improve your relationships and effectiveness in your work or personal life?
4. What barriers prevent you from being a better listener, and how can you overcome them?

Learning: The Path to Continuous Improvement

In the NFL, with only 16 games in a regular season, there's no room for complacency. Every week presents a new challenge, a new opponent to study, and new strategies to master. In this environment, the ability to learn quickly and effectively isn't just an advantage—it's a necessity.

In Indianapolis, we cultivated a culture of learning that was built around three key elements: asking great questions, executing on the answers, and constant evaluation.

1. **Asking great questions:** We were encouraged to be curious and inquisitive. Coach Dungy often reminded us that there were no foolish questions, and that we can't afford to ask questions on Sundays. This created an environment where everyone felt comfortable seeking clarification or deeper understanding. As Hall of Fame college football coach, Lou Holtz famously said, "I never learned anything by talking. I only learned things when I asked questions."

2. **Execution:** Learning wasn't just about acquiring knowledge—it was about putting that knowledge into practice. We were expected to take what we learned in meetings and film sessions and apply it on the practice field and in games.

3. **Evaluation:** In the NFL, we lived by the mantra "The eye in the sky doesn't lie." Every minute of every practice and game was filmed and analyzed. This allowed us to objectively assess our performance, identify areas for improvement, and track our progress over time. This systematic approach to learning allowed us to continually refine our skills and strategies, giving us a competitive edge throughout the long NFL season.

Another insight from Tony Dungy in his book *Uncommon* says, "The best players and the best teams don't just work hard; they work smart. They are always learning, always growing, always pushing to get better."[3]

Reflective Questions:

1. How can you create an environment in your workplace or personal life that encourages asking questions and seeking understanding?

2. What systems do you have in place to ensure that you're not just learning, but also executing on what you've learned?
3. How do you evaluate your performance and track your progress in various areas of your life?
4. What barriers prevent you from being a more effective learner, and how can you overcome them?

Language: The Power of Clear Communication

In the complex world of professional football, clear and precise communication can mean the difference between victory and defeat. I remember Coach Dungy teaching us that the key to effective communication is not just about what you're saying, but more importantly how you're saying it.

Nowhere was this more evident than in our offensive system under Peyton Manning, which featured one of the most intricate audible systems in NFL history. I called it "the language of Manning," and it taught us a crucial lesson: Every single word matters.

In a single play call, Peyton Manning might say something like "Dice right, ice cream, alert 654 Jose, on nothing." Each of these words had a specific meaning, conveying crucial information to different players on the offense. In this example, one word was more important than the rest. Can you guess which one? "Nothing"! It was the last word added in his huddle delivery. "Nothing" told us that the play didn't exist, and that he was going to try and trick the defense into jumping offsides or at least shift their position and reveal their strategy. "Ice cream" were words that told us he would provide a code word at the line of scrimmage in the form of any flavor of ice cream he chooses, like "chocolate, chocolate," to remind us that the play was on "nothing," so don't move a muscle no matter what he said or did at the line of scrimmage to entice them into making a mistake.

If the opponent jumped offsides we won the moment, and if they only shifted and revealed their strategy we still won, because then our grand master chess player of a quarterback would begin delivering his intricate audible system of words and hand signals telling us exactly what he wanted us to do in order to be successful. It was mentally exhausting but highly effective. This is one of my favorites themes to share in my culture keynote speech because I get to reveal and breakdown the "Language of Manning" in great detail, and yes, I do tell people what his famous code word "Omaha" means!

This experience underscored three key principles of effective communication:

1. **Content:** What am I saying? As a communicator, you need to be crystal clear about the information you're trying to convey.
2. **Purpose:** Why am I saying it? Understanding the goal of your communication helps ensure that your message is focused and relevant.
3. **Delivery:** How am I saying it? Recognizing that people receive and process information differently, try not to communicate out of assumptions but instead focus on elite levels of context. It's important to consider how best to deliver your message for maximum effectiveness.

These principles apply far beyond the football field. Whether you're leading a business team, teaching a class, or communicating with family members, clear and purposeful language is essential for effective interaction and collaboration.

As Tony Dungy writes in *Quiet Strength*, "Communication is the key to success in any relationship, whether it's between a coach and player, a husband and wife, or a parent and child."[4]

Reflective Questions:
1. In your communication, how often do you consider not just what you're saying, but why you're saying it and how you're delivering the message?

2. How can you adapt your communication style to better reach different individuals or groups you interact with?
3. What strategies can you employ to ensure that your message is being received and understood as intended?
4. How might improving your communication skills enhance your effectiveness in your personal and professional life?

Love: The Glue That Binds a Team

Of all the principles we've discussed, perhaps the most powerful—and potentially the most uncomfortable to address in a professional setting—is love. But when we talk about love in the context of team culture, we're not talking about romantic feelings or even friendship in the traditional sense. We're talking about a deep sense of value and respect for each team member as a human being.

In Indianapolis, this principle was encapsulated in our belief that "if we build better men, we get better football players." This philosophy was so central to our culture that it was even engraved on our Super Bowl rings with the word "FAITH"—an acronym for "Freedom for All Individuals to Trust and Hope in each other."

This culture of love and respect was built on three key elements:

1. **Trust:** We fostered an environment where team members could rely on each other both on and off the field.
2. **Commitment:** Each player was expected to give their best effort every day, not just for personal gain, but out of respect for their teammates and coaches.
3. **Unity:** We cultivated a sense of shared purpose and mutual support that went beyond just winning games.

This approach to team building has parallels in successful organizations outside of sports. For example, my brother-in-law Erik Stordahl, who has an MBA from Notre Dame and is a Six

Sigma lean manufacturing expert form Toyota, taught me that the Toyota Way includes a principle called *Ninguen Se Sanshu*, which roughly translates to "love and respect for your employees," but more deeply means "to hold precious that which makes a person human." This is a foundational belief principle of one of the greatest and most successful auto manufacturers in the world.

By treating each team member as a valued individual and fostering strong interpersonal relationships, the Colts created a team that was more than the sum of its parts—a team that was resilient, committed, and unified in its pursuit of excellence.

Another profound thought from Tony Dungy in *Quiet Strength* says, "The secret to success is good leadership, and the secret to good leadership is all about making the lives of your team members or workers better."[5]

Reflective Questions:
1. How can you foster a culture of trust and respect in your workplace or personal relationships?
2. What actions can you take to show that you value the humanity of those around you, beyond their roles or what they can do for you?
3. How might prioritizing interpersonal relationships and mutual respect impact the performance and satisfaction of your team or family?
4. What barriers exist in your environment that prevent the development of deep, respectful relationships, and how can you work to overcome them?

The lessons I learned during my time with the Indianapolis Colts extend far beyond the realm of professional football. They speak to universal truths about leadership, teamwork, and personal growth that can be applied in any context—whether you're running a business, leading a community organization, or simply striving to be the best version of yourself.

The Four Ls—Listening, Learning, Language, and Love—provide a framework for building a culture of excellence, respect, and continuous improvement. By intentionally practicing these principles, we can create environments where individuals feel valued, teams are united, and organizations thrive.

As you reflect on these principles, consider how you might apply them in your own life and work. Remember, culture isn't something that just happens—it's something that's chosen and cultivated through consistent practice and unwavering commitment to shared values.

In the words of my favorite coach, Tony Dungy, from his book *Uncommon*, "Life is about relationships, not accomplishments. It's about investing in people, not impressing people. It's about character, not comfort."[6]

By focusing on building better people—whether they're athletes, employees, students, or family members—we inevitably create better teams, better organizations, and a better world. That's the true power of championship culture.

8

The Culture Creed

IN THE PREVIOUS chapters, we explored the foundational principles of organizational culture and examined how chosen beliefs and values can shape a winning team environment. Now it's time to take the next crucial step in building your championship culture: developing your Culture Creed™.

A Culture Creed is more than just a mission statement or a list of core values. It is a powerful, comprehensive declaration of your organization's beliefs, values, and expectations. It serves as both a guiding light for decision-making and a rallying cry that unites your team around a common purpose. In essence, your Culture Creed becomes the DNA of your organization—the code that shapes every aspect of how you operate and interact.

Our DNA as humans tells the story of our creation. It provides intimate details into the makeup of our cellular identity. One of the most important aspects to developing a Culture Creed is storytelling. Your Culture Creed design should tell the organizational story of your foundational beliefs and values. Remember, inspiration is the key to commitment.

One of my favorite companies in Minnesota is exceptional in how they tell their story. My dear friend Elliott Badzin, whose dad founded the company, is CEO of Factory Motor Parts and has dedicated his life to the perpetuation of his family's story.

I'll never forget the first time I met Elliott. I entered his corner office, and he invited me to sit at a round conversational table near tall glorious windows overlooking the campus of FMP. The first thing I noticed was a large hardcover book in the middle of the table—the story of Factory Motor Parts, "A Forever Company." It is filled with inspirational stories and pictures dating back to the company's inception in 1945 as Elliott Auto Supply Co. Every single page focuses on promoting a culture of family.

Elliott designed a culture focused on family because of the profound significance of his Jewish heritage. The Jewish culture places the highest value on life, family, and the welfare of others. The way in which FMP lives its story differentiates them in the market. They treat their employees like family and truly care about one another.

One small auto supply company founded in 1945 on the north side of Minneapolis has now scaled to over 300 locations across the United States with headquarters in Minnesota, Tel Aviv, and Shanghai, with thousands of team members. Factory Motor Parts has become one of the largest distributors of aftermarket automotive parts and accessories, emphasizing the foundational importance of family while inspiring excellence. Mediocrity is not an option.

Elliott Badzin has shown us what the power of a story can accomplish, especially when you incorporate it into an organizational creed that inspires the beliefs in what you value as a company.

As I highlighted, throughout history, creeds have played a pivotal role in shaping the behavior and commitments of communities. From religious doctrines to national constitutions, creeds have the power to inspire, guide, and transform. In the context of organizational culture, a well-crafted creed can:

- **Provide clarity and direction:** A Culture Creed clearly articulates what your organization stands for, helping to align everyone's efforts toward common goals.

- **Foster unity and belonging:** By expressing shared values and beliefs, a creed creates a sense of community and shared purpose among team members.
- **Guide decision-making:** When faced with difficult choices, team members can turn to the creed for guidance, ensuring decisions align with the organization's core beliefs.
- **Attract and retain talent:** A compelling Culture Creed can serve as a powerful recruitment tool, attracting individuals who resonate with your values and helping to retain those who embody them.
- **Drive performance:** When people understand and believe in the "why" behind their work, they are more likely to go above and beyond in their efforts.

Creating Your Culture Creed: A Step-by-Step Guide

Developing a Culture Creed is not a task to be taken lightly. It requires deep reflection, honest dialogue, and a commitment to authenticity. Here's a step-by-step guide to help you create a powerful Culture Creed for your organization:

Step 1: Reflect on Your Core Beliefs

Start by asking yourself and your leadership team some fundamental questions:

1. What do we believe about our purpose as an organization?
2. What do we believe about our role in the lives of our customers, employees, and community?
3. What do we believe about how work should be done and how people should be treated?
4. What do we believe sets us apart from other organizations in our field?

Take time to discuss these questions in depth. Don't settle for surface-level answers—dig deep to uncover the true beliefs that drive your organization.

Step 2: Identify Your Key Values

Based on your core beliefs, what values symbolize your core beliefs and are most important to your organization? These might include principles like integrity, innovation, teamwork, customer focus, or social responsibility. Aim to identify three to five core values that truly define your organization's character and performance beliefs.

Step 3: Articulate Your Expectations

For each of your core beliefs and values, define specific behaviors and actions that demonstrate that value in practice. For example, if one of your values is "customer focus," you might expect employees to always respond to customer inquiries within 24 hours, or to go above and beyond to solve customer problems.

Step 4: What Your Culture Creed Should Objectively Define

1. What you believe (your core beliefs about performance value principles)
2. Why you believe it (the reasoning and psychology behind your beliefs)
3. How these beliefs should manifest in behavior (your values and expectations)

Here's a simple template you can use:

"We believe [what: core belief], because [why: reason]. Therefore, we value [value] and expect [how: specific behaviors]."

For example: "We believe that every person has inherent worth and potential, because human dignity is universal and inviolable. Therefore, we value respect and expect all team members to treat each other, our customers, and our community with kindness, empathy, and fairness in every interaction."

Step 5: Refine and Polish the Draft of Your Culture Creed

1. Is it clear and concise?
2. Does it truly capture the essence of your organization?
3. Does it inspire and motivate?

Share it with a wider group of employees and gather feedback. Refine and polish until you have a creed that resonates with everyone in your organization.

Bringing Your Culture Creed to Life

Creating your Culture Creed is just the beginning. For it to truly shape your organizational culture, you need to bring it to life in every aspect of your operations.

Here are some strategies for embedding your Culture Creed into the fabric of your organization:

- **Leadership modeling.** As with any aspect of culture, your Culture Creed must start at the top. Leaders at all levels of the organization must embody the beliefs, values, and behaviors outlined in the creed. When leaders consistently model the desired culture, it sends a powerful message throughout the organization.
- **Onboarding and training.** Make your Culture Creed a central part of your onboarding process for new employees. Develop training programs that help employees understand not just what the creed says, but how to apply it in

their daily work. Consider creating scenarios or case studies that allow employees to practice making decisions based on the creed.

- **Regular communication.** Find ways to consistently reinforce your Culture Creed in your internal communications. This could include featuring elements of the creed in company newsletters, creating posters or visual reminders throughout your workspace, or starting meetings with a brief discussion of how the creed applies to the topic at hand.

- **Recognition and rewards.** Develop recognition programs that celebrate employees who exemplify the beliefs, values, and behaviors outlined in your Culture Creed. This could include peer-to-peer recognition systems, regular "culture champion" awards, or incorporating creed-aligned behaviors into your performance review process.

- **Decision-making processes.** Integrate your Culture Creed into your decision-making processes at all levels of the organization. Encourage teams to explicitly consider how potential decisions align with the creed. This ensures that your culture truly guides your actions as an organization.

- **Hiring and promotion.** Use your Culture Creed as a guide in your hiring and promotion processes. Develop interview questions that assess candidates' alignment with your core beliefs and values. Consider how well current employees embody the creed when making promotion decisions.

- **Customer and stakeholder interactions.** Extend your Culture Creed beyond your internal operations to shape how you interact with customers, partners, and other stakeholders. Make sure your external communications and customer service practices align with the beliefs and values expressed in your creed.

- **Regular review and refinement.** Your Culture Creed should be a living document that evolves as your organization grows and changes. Schedule regular reviews (perhaps annually) to assess how well your creed is serving your organization and make refinements as needed.

Culture Creed Case Study

One company that exemplifies the power of a strong Culture Creed is Zappos, the online shoe and clothing retailer. Zappos is renowned for its unique and vibrant company culture, which is encapsulated in its core values:

- Deliver WOW Through Service
- Embrace and Drive Change
- Create Fun and a Little Weirdness
- Be Adventurous, Creative, and Open-Minded
- Pursue Growth and Learning
- Build Open and Honest Relationships with Communication
- Build a Positive Team and Family Spirit
- Do More with Less
- Be Passionate and Determined
- Be Humble

These values aren't just words on a wall at Zappos—they're deeply ingrained in every aspect of the company's operations.

Here's How Zappos Brings Its Culture to Life

- **Hiring for culture fit:** Zappos has a rigorous hiring process that includes a "culture interview" to ensure new hires align with the company's values.

- **Training and development:** All new employees, regardless of position, go through the same four-week training program that heavily emphasizes the company's culture and values.
- **Empowering employees:** Call center employees are encouraged to take as much time as needed with customers and are empowered to make decisions that align with the company's values.
- **Transparency:** Zappos practices radical transparency, sharing financial and operational information with all employees.
- **Fun and quirkiness:** The company encourages fun and self-expression, with offices featuring decorated workspaces, parades, and even a nap room.

The results of this strong culture are clear: Zappos consistently ranks as one of the best places to work, has exceptionally low turnover rates, and is known for its fanatically loyal customers. Zappos CEO Tony Hsieh once said, "Your personal core values define who you are, and a company's core values ultimately define the company's character and brand. For individuals, character is destiny. For organizations, culture is destiny." This statement encapsulates the power of a well-defined and lived Culture Creed.

By clearly articulating its beliefs, values, and embedding them deeply into every aspect of its operations, Zappos has created a distinct and powerful organizational culture that drives its success.

Overcoming Challenges in Implementing Your Culture Creed

While the benefits of a strong Culture Creed are clear, implementing and maintaining it can present challenges. Here are some common obstacles you might face and strategies to overcome them:

- **Resistance to change challenge:** Employees, especially long-term ones, may resist changes to the existing culture.

  Solution: Involve employees in the process of creating and refining the Culture Creed. Communicate clearly about why the creed is important and how it will benefit everyone. Provide support and training to help employees adapt to new expectations.

- **Inconsistent application challenge:** Different departments or leaders may interpret or apply the Culture Creed inconsistently.

  Solution: Provide clear guidelines and examples of how the creed should be applied in various situations. Regularly discuss and share best practices across the organization. Hold leaders accountable for consistently modeling creed-aligned behaviors.

- **Cynicism or skepticism challenge:** Employees may view the Culture Creed as just another corporate initiative that will soon be forgotten.

  Solution: Demonstrate long-term commitment by consistently reinforcing the creed and tying it to tangible actions and decisions. Celebrate and share stories of how the creed is making a positive difference in the organization.

- **Lack of measurement challenge:** It can be difficult to measure the impact of the Culture Creed, leading to questions about its value.

  Solution: Develop specific metrics tied to your Culture Creed, such as employee engagement scores, customer satisfaction ratings, or specific behavioral indicators. Regularly assess and report on these metrics to demonstrate the creed's impact.

A well-crafted and consistently applied Culture Creed has the power to transform your organization. It can align your team around a shared purpose, guide decision-making at all levels, attract and retain top talent, and ultimately drive superior perfor-mance. Remember, your Culture Creed is not just a statement—it's a commitment. It's a promise you make to your employees, your customers, and your community about who you are and how you operate.

Living up to this promise requires ongoing effort, dedication, and sometimes difficult choices. But the rewards—a cohesive team, a positive work environment, satisfied customers, and sustainable success—are well worth the investment.

As you embark on the journey of creating and implementing your Culture Creed, keep in mind the words of organizational culture expert Edgar Schein: "The only thing of real importance that leaders do is to create and manage culture."[1]

Your Culture Creed is your most powerful tool for creating and managing a culture of excellence. Use it wisely, live it con-sistently, and watch as it transforms your organization from the inside out.

Here are several pages from the Culture Creed I developed for the private equity company in Minnesota in which I have had the role of chief culture officer. It spotlights the True North corporate Culture Creed, a private equity company with a portfolio consisting of over 28 companies, spanning 9 different industries.

True North's nonnegotiable belief is built on the power of servant leadership. Founder and CEO Brian Slipka is dedicated to building a culture that strives to put the human condition first. Slipka's leadership and passion for small to mid-size businesses has created a specific community that he can focus on inspiring, developing, and managing toward a chosen belief and value strategy and system.

Here is the language I developed for the True North Culture Creed, along with an example of how I transformed the value principle of Integrity into a practicable belief system.

At True North Equity Partners, we believe that what we believe directs how we behave and that Culture is the Human Condition at work. We Believe Culture is the Leader's choice and that choice should positively impact the human condition of all who come in contact with our brand.

We believe that Culture is an objective tool built upon What People Believe, Why People Believe, and How People Behave. The practicing of a chosen belief system is what inspires people and communities to work together in unity and purpose. Every individual has intrinsic beliefs that guide their behaviors and results in the production of culture. In essence, you will always have a culture by design or default. So why not design it?

At True North, our eight-pillar belief system symbolizes essential truths we believe define who we are as an organization and leadership team. Our culture design has been intentionally chosen to create an ecosystem that is vibrant and healthy, resulting in sustainable, positive outcomes. We will practice the True North Culture across all True North businesses, replicating a shared belief system that will unify, inspire, and serve the community well. Lastly, we will help direct the culture through providing leaders and True North organizations an educational and developmental platform that will empower them in practicing the Champion Culture of True North Equity Partners.

The True North Creed:

We believe practicing **Integrity** will guide us in developing more meaningful relationships with our clients. We believe practicing **Trust** will create profitable and long-lasting partnerships with the people and organizations we serve. We believe practicing **Humility** is the key ingredient in serving well all who come in contact with our brand. We believe practicing **Wisdom** will provide a peaceful, nurturing, and reassuring environment through sound discernment. We believe practicing **Execution** will help us grow efficiently. We believe practicing **Accountability** will help develop future leaders. We believe practicing **Commitment** will produce unity and team success. Lastly, we believe practicing **Love** will empower us to positively impact every life that comes in contact with True North Equity Partners.

Within each pillar are multiple subcultures. These are additional beliefs that are directly associated with the foundational pillar. Each belief has a specific meaning and purpose we will define and develop. Within the development of the shared belief system, we will create practicable applications that will help you and your teams grow if you choose to utilize them. These applications should also inspire originality and help the leaders and their team members create their own forms of culture development that is best suitable for their unique location sub-culture.

In order to achieve ultimate success in sports, athletes practice for the majority of their careers while their performance constitutes a minority of their time. It may be the only industry in the world with that performance model. Practicing anything is the key to becoming great at it. This philosophy is why we believe that Culture is deeper than words found in our mission, vision, and value statements. It is found in an elected set of foundational beliefs that we not only identify with, but also choose to practice. This enables us to hold each other accountable to grow in each belief, improving our human condition and resulting in our best performance.

The What:

Integrity—"Soundness of moral character; honest, and above reproach."[2]

The Why:

At True North we believe that integrity is the key to building the strongest team possible and creating a business that will experience growth and provide an essential social impact on every person who comes in contact with our brand. A person with integrity is someone who behaves in a manner that places the highest level of importance on doing the right thing. They practice principles consistently that produce fruit, like trust and commitment. Integrity is a key factor in building deep and meaningful relationships that are grounded in respect. When you practice a culture of integrity, especially through the hiring process, you will create teams that will work as hard as they can for the betterment of the team, not just themselves.

Integrity requires honesty, a characteristic that seems obvious but can be a quality much harder to come by than expected. Honesty also builds trust and trust improves operational efficiency, relationship management, and customer appreciation. A person with integrity has strong self-awareness that allows them to understand the importance of responsibility and accountability. Taking responsibility for your actions is an essential quality in leadership that affects the entire team positively because it reveals a direct correlation to what you believe and it helps others see you as someone that is dependable.

Culture is the leader's choice, which is why the leadership of TNEP believes that Integrity is essential to improving the human condition at work. Let's commit to practice a culture of Integrity.

The How:

An example of how Integrity is practiced in the workplace is always striving to exceed expectations, like finishing your work ahead of expectation and with excellence. There will be times when that doesn't happen, and practicing Integrity would be leading with honesty and taking responsibility for your circumstance. In the financial industry, Integrity is practiced by staying true to one's fiduciary commitments. Taking ownership of your performance is critical and is directly connected to an individual's character and honesty.

How to develop integrity in the workplace:
1. Provide clear and concise performance expectations that give your team members the best chance to prove themselves and win for you.
2. Create team building exercises designed to address moral responsibilities that empower the individual to make good decisions for themselves and others around them.
3. Encourage team members to serve the community on their own outside of the organizations. This will inspire humility and honesty.

True North Mergers and Acquisitions and Sunbelt Business Advisors, which are a part of the True North family of companies, have also chosen to make culture their competitive edge in an industry that struggles with trust. Chairman Brian Slipka and CEO Chris Jones committed to going further and deeper than most companies in their industry to inspire, articulate, and practice chosen belief and value principles that are designed to enhance internal relationships, but equally important to serve their clients and community with unbelievable hospitality.

I was recently onboarding a new advisor at True North Mergers and Acquisitions. During the culture training, the advisor who came from the largest healthcare organization in the world shared that our companies Culture Creed was one of the primary reasons why he accepted the position. He explained how unique and powerful it was to experience a manuscript that inspirationally and educationally clarified the organizational culture.

This affirmed my hopes. When you make culture more than just aspirational words on a website and instead develop a culture training product, not only will you ensure a more successful culture integration process, but you will also have a profound culture marketing and business development tool to differentiate yourself in a competitive marketplace.

These are two companies you can trust with confidence when buying or selling your businesses.

The goal of the Culture Creed is to enhance organizational culture knowledge and experience producing wisdom. Wisdom is a quality that is hard to come by because it depends upon multiple influencers working together to enhance your decision-making capabilities, which includes how you choose to behave. I believe that wisdom is found at the intersection of knowledge and experience.

The Culture Creed will be your inspirational and educational platform, ensuring that all applicants and employees fully understand the culture of the organization and how their behaviors should reflect the nonnegotiable beliefs and values of the company. The Creed will also support your human development strategies and systems by providing a game plan that always strives to develop people toward the overall culture belief and value principles.

When you develop, launch, and practice a Culture Creed successfully, you will empower the applicant to choose the culture that is best for them while increasing the organization's ability to protect itself from hiring an individual outside of natural culture alignment.

9

The Secret Sauce

FOR LEADERS OF any organization one truism of culture always exists: "You will have one." Whether by design or default, culture always happens. Perspectives on culture and culture management differ among leaders. Some see culture as ethereal: hard to define and even harder to manage. Others take a differing position: culture is a principal asset of the organization; it is tangible and marketable, and it can and should be led and managed.

A couple of years ago I met an unique and passionate CEO of a construction company in Tacoma, Washington. Clif Peterson is unique because he founded, built, and scaled a highly successful construction company on the foundation of "Joy."

In fact, it was more than just the foundation; it is the actual brand title of the company: "Joy Inc." I was fascinated by his choice of words used to market and describe his company.

We built a fast friendship and began to work together. Clif invited me to speak to his team of construction workers out in Tacoma. During my time with "Joy Inc." I discovered the secret sauce to Clif's culture recipe. He poured out love and mentorship onto these gritty, hardworking blue-collar employees in ways I have never seen before.

As CEO, Clif personally mentors every single one of his employees, spending hours a month with them focusing on leadership development and learning. Clif also has a reading program where he gives bonuses to team members who read leadership books and draft a report on their findings and experience. Clif believes that you should never ask someone to do something that you won't do yourself, which is why he committed to reading one new book each week. Yes, you heard me correctly, he reads 52 books a year!

While I was speaking to his team about building championship culture, I was stunned to see every single one of them taking notes. After the session I shared with Clif that I had never seen that attention to detail before out of a group. He explained that it was by design. Clif awards his team members when they take thorough notes, learning from speakers and experts, and then turning them in.

Clif Peterson has one singular passion and that is to inspire and distribute joy into the lives of all of his team members, clients, vendors, and the community he lives in. He has also turned his "Joy Inc." brand into some of the coolest company apparel I have seen. In fact my family and I wear his message of joy whenever we can with his "Joy Inc." hats, shirts, and hoodies. When you design culture well, it becomes a material product that enhances marketing and business development.

We can all learn something from CEO Clif Peterson and how he has chosen to build a culture by design, and not accept a culture by default. He taught me that even a belief like "Joy" can be deliberately constructed as the primary strategy of a company, supported by practicable systems.

The theme of this chapter is a culture by design. Dr. Zismer's foundational premise here is "Culture is the leaders' choice." Culture can be defined, designed, deployed, and directed as the foundation for success of any organization. As entrepreneur and bestselling author Gino Wickman states, "Great companies that stand the test of time have a strong culture, and that culture is intentional."[1]

A positive and constructive culture is what happens in an organization when leadership satisfies the human condition's need for inspiration, aspiration, and performance beliefs within an environment of trust, faith, and confidence in the purpose of the work to be done. Let's focus on three core themes that are essential to perfecting your culture recipe.

The Intentionality of Culture

Leaders must be intentional about the culture of their organization. Common culture is embraced as the foundation for success. The operative term here is "common culture"—a culture common to and shared by the members of the organization. Will Guidara, restaurateur and author of *Unreasonable Hospitality*, emphasizes this point: "Culture isn't something that just happens. It's something you build, intentionally, every single day."[2]

Let's take a side trip into another industry: the NFL. The parallels between successful NFL teams and successful businesses are striking:

- Elite, highly skilled, trained, and practiced professionals
- High-intensity, high-tempo environments
- High financial stakes
- Highly competitive
- High risk
- Precision execution, audibles, hand-offs, fumbles, wins, and losses
- High brand value

As legendary NFL coach Vince Lombardi said, "Individual commitment to a group effort—that is what makes a team work, a company work, a society work, a civilization work."[3]

The Anatomy of a Culture Plan

Leaders seeking to set the foundation for a high-functioning organization should consider the following 10 component parts:

1. The business description
2. The branding and brand positioning
3. The mission, vision, belief, and business strategy
4. The value propositions
5. The compact (shared organizational values and principles)
6. Standards of practice
7. The functioning of "the team"
8. Due process
9. After-hours and off-campus behaviors
10. Citizenship expectations

These 10 points represent the foundation of the "culture map" for an organization. This work is not the endpoint for the leaders. It is the beginning.

The Role of Leaders and the Psychology of Culture

The existence of written statements regarding an organization's commitment to culture is necessary, but not sufficient for success. Culture must be lived daily by its leaders with reverence and fidelity. As Bill Belichick, one of the most successful NFL coaches, puts it, "On a team, it's not the strength of the individual players, but it is the strength of the unit and how they all function together."[4]

Leaders of organizations should consider "integrality" as a principal goal of culture development. Here, "integrality" is defined as "essential to completeness,"[5] or moving toward wholeness, or the inclusion of a family. Tom Landry, another legendary NFL coach, reinforces this idea: "Leadership is getting someone to do what they don't want to do, to achieve what they want to achieve."[6]

Over my time working with Dr. Daniel Zismer, we developed some core requirements for leaders to embrace as they consider the right strategy for how to begin transforming their culture.

1. Culture is the leader's choice.
2. Culture matters.
3. You will have a culture, like it or not.
4. Culture can be decided, designed, deployed, and directed.
5. Culture is tangible, it is real, and it is perhaps the most important asset of the organization.
6. Culture will move an organization positively toward mission-focused goals or it will be the indomitable force that prevents mission goal attainment.
7. Culture is the only characteristic of the organization that matters to your employees; good people can find "a job" elsewhere.
8. Culture is where leaders should dedicate the majority of their time, efforts, and organizational resources. Leaders are not fired for spending too much time on culture.
9. Elite organizations are built on elite cultures.
10. The best and brightest across professions are attracted to, and remain committed to, organizations with cultures that hold fidelity to an intrinsically moral, ethical, and respectable and accountable culture.

As my coach Tony Dungy eloquently puts it: "The secret to success is good leadership, and good leadership is all about making the lives of your team members or workers better."[7]

There was no greater leader on our team than Hall of Fame Quarterback Peyton Manning. Peyton had the rare ability to enhance every player's productivity. Manning accomplished this through his own elite gifts and talents as a quarterback, but he also used the power of psychology to distribute affirming performance opportunities and emboldening audible messages.

I will never forget this play. It was the third quarter of Super Bowl XLI and the pressure to score was immense. The rain had become a consistent wall of water. We were yards away from entering the "redzone," which locates our offense within 25 yards of the end zone and a potential touchdown.

It was third down and 8 yards to go for a first down, which would ensure our arrival into the redzone. On this specific play the formation required that I was positioned in the back field like a running back, standing directly to Peyton's left.

The Chicago Bears had lined up in a formation that we had prepared for. Their All-Pro, 6-foot 5-inch, 265-pound middle linebacker Brian Urlacher had run into the A gap, which is adjacent to the offensive center. He wanted us to believe that he was going to blitz, which means he would leave his defensive position on the field in order to sprint at the quarterback to achieve a "sack," which is a tackle on the quarterback.

One of the strongest elements of Peyton's reputation was his elite level of game preparation. No one, and I mean no one, out-prepared Peyton Manning.

When Manning saw Brian Urlacher lined up in the A gap, because of the amount of film study he had applied to this game, he knew that Brian Urlacher was not going to attack but instead fake the blitz.

As our savant quarterback realized the Bears' strategy, he knew exactly which play he would choose to take advantage of the Chicago Bears' weakness. That play was coming to me.

What makes this even more intense was that the play clock was counting down from 30 seconds and now stood at 5 seconds, now 4, now 3 seconds. In that moment Peyton leaned over to me and said "Tech"—a nickname he had given to me—"Urlacher is faking the blitz; get open, I'm coming to you!"

In the one second remaining before the ball had to be snapped, all I could think was holy crap, how about that for pressure! Your

Hall of Fame quarterback tells you to get open because he's throwing the ball to you.

The ball was snapped, and sure enough as Peyton expected, Brian Urlacher did not blitz but instead dropped back into pass coverage. I released and sprinted toward the small opening in the "A" gap between the center and the left guard. I burst through the hole, running straight up the field for 5 yards, then I made my cut.

I planted my left foot hard into the rain-soaked turf. Thankfully my cleats dug in deep, providing the stability needed to make a 90-degree turn to my right. I dashed out of my break and turned to look for the ball. Peyton had already made the throw, and time immediately became slow motion. I can still remember seeing the rainwater fly off of the spiraling football as it soared toward me in perfect location.

I made the pivotal catch and instantly turned up field. As my head circled to find my destination, there standing on the first down line like a mountain screaming "I dare you" is Chicago linebacker Brian Urlacher. I knew in that moment I had a choice to make, and it was going to hurt!

I gripped the ball as hard as I could in preparation for the epic collision that was about to transpire. I lowered my pads and ran as hard as I could into this giant human, barreling through his outside shoulder and landing on the turf just past the first down target.

That first down put our team in scoring position, and we were able to put points on the scoreboard, giving our team the lead over the Chicago Bears. From that moment on we never looked back. We finished the game with a score of 29–17, and became World Champions!

So what's the leadership lesson? As I look back on that momentous play from my career I realized something very special. My quarterback Peyton Manning trusted me. He could have thrown the ball to three or four other players who were pro-bowlers, and future Hall of Famer's but he chose me. As the seconds counted down he leaned over to me and was truly saying, Ben, I believe in you, I trust you will get open, make the catch, and get us the first down.

Peyton's actions as a leader, enhanced my performance on the field but more importantly empowered me as a man. His leadership style was focused on developing team unity and morale even in hostile environments.

Which is why building a championship culture is not just about creating a pleasant work environment. It's about creating a cohesive, high-performing team that consistently achieves its goals. It's about fostering an environment where every team member feels valued, motivated, and aligned with the organization's mission. As leaders, it's our responsibility to foster this culture intentionally and consistently. Remember, culture isn't just part of the game: it is the game.

10

Performance versus Aspiration

ORGANIZATIONAL CULTURE IS fundamentally shaped by the beliefs and values that are espoused and practiced by leadership and employees alike. However, there is a critical distinction between values that are aspirational—what a company hopes to achieve—and those that are performance-based—what is actively being achieved and what leadership behaviors are actually experienced by all team members most consistently.

Early in 2023 I was executive coaching a portfolio manager in one of the companies I was working with as a culture executive. During our sessions I discovered a vital truth that is crucial to understand, if you only use aspirational beliefs and values without any system of behavioral accountability, then leadership will consistently fail to behave in a manner reflecting those principles. Why? Because we are all imperfect humans. This can create an experience of leadership hypocrisy in the workplace, which ultimately leads to distrust and resignation.

In this manager's vulnerability I learned of their deep frustration about how executive leadership was behaving inconsistently with regard to the company's Culture Creed, which was highly aspirational by design. The manager questioned, "How can a company that espouses principles like integrity, respect, and love instead treat its employees with dishonesty, contempt, and hostility?"

87

It was in that question I realized the significance of building organizational culture on the foundation of straightforward performance beliefs and values that clearly define the behaviors that employees will consistently experience from their leaders. Synonymously we must also identify the beliefs and values that we will strive and aspire to achieve. That fuses the power between a culture of execution and a culture of hope.

This analysis examines the differences between creating a culture based on performance versus aspirational beliefs and values, highlighting the benefits of performance-driven culture while acknowledging the role of aspirations in driving continuous improvement.

The Tension between Aspirational and Performance-Based Beliefs and Values

While aspirational beliefs and values can inspire employees, they can also create significant workplace tension when not aligned with reality. For example, a company may tout "work-life balance" as a core value, but in practice, employees are expected to work long hours and be available on weekends. This disconnect can lead to frustration, cynicism, and decreased morale.

As organizational culture expert Edgar Schein notes, "What leaders pay attention to, measure, and control on a regular basis is the most powerful way to communicate what they believe in and care about."[1] When leaders' actions contradict stated values, it erodes trust and credibility.

The Power of Performance-Based Beliefs and Values

Performance-based values, grounded in current practices and behaviors, offer several advantages:

- **Authenticity:** They reflect the true state of the organization, promoting transparency and trust.

- **Clarity:** They provide clear, actionable guidance on expected behaviors.
- **Accountability:** They emphasize measurable outcomes and results.

Leadership expert Jim Collins emphasizes the importance of this approach: "The best leaders don't set out to create a great culture. They set out to create a great company, and the culture emerges as a result of that quest."[2]

The Benefits of Leading through Performance Beliefs and Values

Organizations that prioritize performance-based values often experience:

- Increased trust and credibility
- Higher employee engagement and lower turnover
- Greater adaptability and resilience
- Sustainable long-term success

As organizational psychologist Adam Grant notes, "The culture of a workplace—an organization's values, norms and practices—has a huge impact on our happiness and success."[3]

While aspirational values can inspire and motivate, building a culture primarily on performance-based beliefs and values creates a solid foundation for organizational success. By grounding culture in current realities while still aspiring to improve, companies can foster trust, clarity, and sustainable growth.

As leaders strive to create high-performing organizations, they should focus on aligning stated beliefs and values with actual behaviors, using aspirations as a guide for continuous improvement rather than an unrealistic standard.

Let's dive into some real-world examples of how successful organizations blend performance-based values with aspirational goals to create a powerful cultural framework.

Microsoft: Transforming Culture through Growth Mindset

When Satya Nadella took the helm as CEO of Microsoft in 2014, he orchestrated a significant shift in the company's culture paradigm. Moving away from a "know-it-all" mentality, Nadella championed a "learn-it-all" mindset. This transformation wasn't just about changing slogans; it was about reimagining the very fabric of Microsoft's organizational culture.

Performance Focus

Accountability and collaboration: Under Nadella's guidance, Microsoft sharpened its focus on measurable outcomes and cross-functional teamwork. This approach ensured that the company's objectives were not only crystal clear but also within reach.

Aspirational Focus

Growth mindset: Nadella introduced the concept of a growth mindset, encouraging employees to view challenges as opportunities, criticism as constructive feedback, and setbacks as steppingstones to success. This aspirational value became the cornerstone of Microsoft's cultural metamorphosis, fueling innovation and resilience.

Patagonia: Embedding Environmental Responsibility

Patagonia, the outdoor clothing giant, has woven environmental sustainability into its very DNA. This core belief serves as both a performance metric and an aspirational goal, influencing every decision from supply chain management to product development.

Performance Focus

Sustainability and transparency: Patagonia's business model is built on a foundation of sustainable sourcing and production.

The company prides itself on supply chain transparency and continuously strives to minimize its environmental footprint, setting concrete, measurable targets.

Aspirational Focus

Environmental activism: Patagonia's ambitions extend beyond its own operations. The company aspires to be a catalyst for change, inspiring others to join the fight against environmental degradation. This commitment is exemplified by initiatives like the "1% for the Planet" program, where Patagonia donates 1% of its sales to environmental causes, setting an example for corporate responsibility.

Google: Balancing Innovation with Performance

Google, now under the Alphabet Inc. umbrella, has cultivated a unique culture that strikes a delicate balance between performance-driven excellence and the relentless pursuit of innovation. The company's famous "20% time" policy, which encourages employees to dedicate a fifth of their time to passion projects, has led to groundbreaking products like Gmail and AdSense.

Performance Focus

Data-driven decision-making: At its core, Google's culture is anchored in performance metrics and data analytics. This ensures that all decisions, no matter how innovative, are grounded in measurable outcomes.

Aspirational Focus

Innovation and creativity: Google fosters a culture where innovation isn't just encouraged; it's expected. By allowing employees to explore ideas beyond their immediate job descriptions, Google has created an environment where creativity thrives, solidifying its position as a technology leader.

The world of professional sports also offers some compelling examples of how performance-based values and aspirational goals can create a winning culture.

New England Patriots: The "Do Your Job" Philosophy

Under the leadership of head coach Bill Belichick, the New England Patriots have become a dynasty in the NFL. The team's culture is built on the deceptively simple yet profoundly impactful principle of "Do Your Job," emphasizing personal accountability and role mastery.

Performance Focus

Accountability and precision: The "Do Your Job" mantra is more than just a catchy phrase; it's a performance standard. Players are expected to understand their roles in microscopic detail and execute them flawlessly.

Aspirational Focus

Pursuit of excellence: While the focus is on individual performance, the overarching aspiration is team excellence. Belichick's approach pushes players to continually raise the bar, contributing to the team's remarkable success and multiple Super Bowl victories.

San Antonio Spurs: Values-Driven Success

Under the guidance of coach Gregg Popovich, the San Antonio Spurs have built a reputation for their values-driven approach to team management. The Spurs' culture is a carefully crafted blend of respect, selflessness, and an unwavering commitment to improvement.

Performance Focus

Teamwork and discipline: The Spurs emphasize a team-first mentality and uncompromising discipline. Each player understands their role within the larger team structure, contributing to the Spurs' consistent success and five NBA championships.

Aspirational Focus

Respect and selflessness: Popovich has cultivated a culture where mutual respect and selflessness are paramount. This aspirational value creates an environment where team success takes precedence over individual glory, fostering strong team cohesion and sustained excellence.

All Blacks Rugby Team: The Legacy of the Haka

New Zealand's national rugby team, the All Blacks, are renowned for their commitment to excellence both on and off the field. The Haka, a traditional Māori war dance performed before each match, embodies both performance and aspirational values, symbolizing strength, unity, and an unyielding pursuit of victory.

Performance Focus

Excellence and precision: The All Blacks' success is rooted in a culture of uncompromising excellence. Players are expected to perform at their peak in every match and training session, a standard that has made them one of the most formidable teams in rugby history.

Aspirational Focus

Respect for tradition and legacy: The Haka is more than a pregame ritual; it's a powerful symbol of the team's respect for tradition and their aspiration to honor their predecessors. This aspirational value drives the All Blacks to maintain their status as world leaders in rugby while serving as ambassadors for New Zealand's rich cultural heritage.

Perform with Aspiration

Recognizing the importance of articulating both performance and aspirational values was something I only learned through actual corporate coaching experiences.

These examples vividly illustrate how leading organizations and teams can successfully lead with performance-based beliefs and values with aspirational goals to forge a balanced and effective culture. In the corporate world, giants like Microsoft and Google demonstrate how emphasizing accountability and measurable outcomes can coexist with a culture of innovation and continuous learning. In the arena of professional sports, teams like the New England Patriots and the All Blacks showcase the power of precision and discipline while nurturing a culture of excellence and respect.

Each underscores a crucial lesson: a well-rounded approach to organizational culture—one that is firmly grounded in current performance culture clarity and metrics while constantly reaching for new heights—can lead to sustained success, high levels of engagement, and robust team morale. By striking this delicate balance, these organizations have not only achieved remarkable success but have also created legacies that extend far beyond their immediate spheres of influence.

Understanding the difference between defining your culture through performance or aspirational beliefs and values will help you better manage the realities of workplace hypocrisy that can so easily begin to create toxic attitudes that impact team morale and performance.

At the end of the day, healthy culture will not grow and thrive without the most essential quality: practice!

11

Practice, Practice, Practice!

COACH TONY DUNGY's philosophy was that we would out-practice and out-prepare every other team in the NFL. He accomplished this elite practice strategy by installing twice as many plays in a practice than you would perform in a game.

In fact, we would never condition during the season with traditional sprints, but instead we might run 120 plus plays in our Tuesday and Wednesday practices. Remember, an NFL game on average spotlights between 65 and 75 plays. When you spend your week running twice as many plays in practice, then your endurance during a game feels that much stronger.

Another central practice technique was our on the field "walk-through" session. This practice time was an hour in length, and we would literally walk through every single play that was installed during that morning's meetings. That would allow us as an offense to see all possible defensive schemes we might face from our opponents.

The slow-motion quality of the work embedded our offensive strategy deep within our minds, enhancing our memory recall, which would prove to be critical to our gameday success.

After finishing the walk-through practice we would then separate into our individual position meetings and evaluate the film of the walk-through session. It was riveting! Okay, maybe not.

Watching a walk-through practice can definitely challenge your sleep habits but if you're paying attention, it reveals all of the scenarios and potential challenges you will face against your opponent on gameday.

Practice is what makes every team, in every organization, in every industry, more successful. Imagine if we took that approach toward human development.

In the realm of professional sports and business, there's a stark contrast in how time is allocated between practice and performance. This disparity offers valuable insights, particularly when comparing the National Football League (NFL) to the corporate world. By examining these differences, we can glean important lessons about the value of practice and its potential to transform business performance.

The NFL: A Testament to the Power of Practice

In the NFL, the ratio of practice time to game time is staggering. As legendary coach Vince Lombardi once said, "Practice does not make perfect. Only perfect practice makes perfect." This philosophy is deeply ingrained in the NFL culture, where players spend an overwhelming majority of their careers honing their skills off the field.

Let's break down the numbers:

1. **Practice Time:**

   Offseason workouts: ~300 hours per year

   Training camp: ~200 hours per year

   In-season practices: ~480 hours per year

   Total: Approximately 980 hours per year

2. **Game Performance Time:**

   Regular season: ~187 minutes (17 games × 11 minutes of active play per game)

Playoffs: ~22 minutes (assuming 2 games)

Total: Approximately 209 minutes or 3.5 hours per year

Over an average NFL career of 3.3 years, this translates to:

Total career practice time: ~3,234 hours

Total career game performance time: ~11.55 hours

The practice-to-performance ratio in the NFL is a staggering 280:1. For every hour spent playing in games, NFL players dedicate 280 hours to practice and preparation. As Tom Brady, one of the most successful quarterbacks in NFL history, once said, "I think that at the start of a game, you're always playing to win, and then maybe if you're ahead late in the game, you start playing not to lose. The true competitors, though, are the ones who always play to win."[1]

This mindset of constant improvement through practice is what separates the great players from the good ones.

The Corporate World: The Issue of Performance over Practice

In stark contrast to the NFL, the corporate world often emphasizes performance over practice. Let's examine the typical time allocation in a business environment:

1. **Work Time:**
   Standard work hours: ~2,080 hours per year
   With overtime: Up to ~2,320 hours per year

2. **Human Development Time:**
   First year: ~120–150 hours (including onboarding)
   Subsequent years: ~80–110 hours

The human development (practice) to work ratio in business at its highest is 1:29. For every hour spent on human development, employees spend 29 hours working or performing. This imbalance reveals a significant opportunity for businesses to improve their approach to employee development and organizational performance.

The NFL provides some amazing insights and strategies that businesses can use to develop a culture that drives performance and success.

1. **Prioritize practice and skill development.** NFL teams understand that gameday performance is a direct result of countless hours of practice. Businesses should adopt a similar mindset, allocating more time and resources to employee training and skill development.

   As basketball legend Michael Jordan once said, "You can practice shooting eight hours a day, but if your technique is wrong, then all you become is very good at shooting the wrong way." This emphasizes the importance of not just practicing, but practicing effectively.

2. **Create a culture of continuous improvement.** In the NFL, players and coaches are constantly analyzing their performance and looking for ways to improve. This culture of continuous improvement should be emulated in the business world. Jack Welch, former CEO of General Electric, echoed this sentiment when he said, "An organization's ability to learn, and translate that learning into action rapidly, is the ultimate competitive advantage."[2]

3. **Invest in long-term development.** NFL teams invest heavily in player development, knowing that it will pay off in future seasons. Similarly, businesses should view employee development as a long-term investment rather than a short-term cost. Warren Buffett, one of the most

successful investors of all time, advises, "Someone's sitting in the shade today because someone planted a tree a long time ago."[3] This principle applies equally to developing human capital in business.

4. **Balance individual and team development.** In football, players work on individual skills while also practicing team strategies. Businesses should strive for a similar balance, focusing on both individual employee growth and team cohesion. Phil Jackson, legendary NBA coach, emphasized this balance: "The strength of the team is each individual member. The strength of each member is the team."[4]

5. **Measure and analyze performance.** NFL teams meticulously analyze game footage and practice performance to identify areas for improvement. Businesses should implement robust performance measurement and analysis systems to drive continuous improvement. Peter Drucker, management consultant and author, famously said, "What gets measured gets managed." This principle is as true in business as it is in sports.

Practice is imperative. The stark contrast between the NFL's practice-to-performance ratio and that of the corporate world highlights a significant opportunity for businesses. By learning from the NFL's emphasis on practice and preparation, organizations can develop their people toward their best performance.

As legendary football coach Bear Bryant once said, "It's not the will to win that matters—everyone has that. It's the will to prepare to win that matters." This philosophy, when applied to business, can lead to transformative results.

Businesses and organizations should take a page from the NFL playbook and recognize that practice is essential for developing people toward their best performance. By dedicating more time and resources to employee development, creating a culture of continuous improvement, and focusing on long-term growth, companies can unlock their full potential and achieve sustainable success.

In the words of famed basketball coach John Wooden, "It's what you learn after you know it all that counts."[5] The business world would do well to embrace this mindset, making ongoing learning and development a cornerstone of their organizational culture.

By shifting the balance toward more practice and development time, businesses can create a workforce that is not just prepared for today's challenges, but is continuously evolving to meet the demands of tomorrow. In doing so, they'll be better positioned to outperform their competitors and achieve lasting success in an ever-changing business landscape.

12

Data-Driven Culture

IN THE HIGH-STAKES world of the NFL, teams are constantly searching for any advantage in acquiring top talent. The days of relying solely on game tapes and gut instincts are long gone. Today's NFL front offices employ a sophisticated blend of performance metrics, psychological assessments, and behavioral data to make informed decisions about potential draft picks and free agent signings.

When I joined the Colts I had a meeting with Chris Polian, the director of scouting at the time and also the son of General Manager Bill Polian. We met in the scouting office and what I saw was astounding. All four walls in the large square meeting room were transformed into white boards covered with series of systematic data templates designed for recording every possible player statistic.

Each wall resembled a physical Excel spreadsheet and every section was filled with players' names and specific numbers connected to their performance. I had never seen this degree of sports performance information in my life. Each data point was intentionally considered to prioritize the organization's talent acquisition process.

Another unique data theme was focused on each player's integrity and character as a man. This was a design philosophy developed and practiced by Bill Polian. He believed that if a player's life reflected qualities such as doing the right thing, perseverance, academic success, leadership ability, and dependability, these qualities would transfer onto the field.

Polian said he would rather draft a third- to fifth-round player who was the captain of their team and had earned a college degree than a first- or second-round pick with all the elite talent in the world but with a significant history of off-the-field problems. Drafting players who had natural alignment toward the Colts' beliefs and values ensured a greater opportunity for team success and sustainability.

As Bill Belichick, head coach of the New England Patriots, once said, "We look at everything. There's no single thing that's the answer. You try to get as much information as you can and make the best decision possible."[1]

Here's a look at some NFL performance data designed to inspire you toward the importance of how data can be used to support a performance culture.

Physical Metrics

1. Combine statistics: The NFL Scouting Combine remains a crucial source of standardized physical data. Teams analyze these metrics to gauge a prospect's raw athleticism and potential.
2. Game film analysis: While the eye test still matters, teams now use advanced software to break down game film and extract detailed performance data.
3. Advanced analytics: Metrics like Expected Points Added (EPA) and Pro Football Focus (PFF) grades offer a more nuanced view of a player's impact.

Positional-Specific Data

1. Quarterbacks: Teams dive deep into decision-making metrics, pressure performance, and accuracy under various conditions.
2. Wide receivers: Separation metrics, catch radius, and yards after catch (YAC) help paint a complete picture of a receiver's skillset.
3. Defensive players: Modern analytics track metrics like tackle efficiency, pass-rush win rate, and coverage grades to evaluate defensive talent.

Psychological Data

1. Wonderlic test: While its importance has diminished, this test still provides a baseline for cognitive abilities.
2. Cognitive processing speed: New tests focus on how quickly players can process information and make decisions on the field.

Psychological Profiling

1. Personality tests: These assessments help teams gauge how a player might fit into their culture and handle the pressures of the NFL.
2. Mental toughness and grit: Teams are increasingly valuing mental resilience and work ethic alongside physical talents.

Behavioral Assessment

1. Behavioral interviews: In-depth interviews help teams assess a player's character, leadership potential, and ability to work within a team structure.
2. Character evaluation: Off-field behavior and social media presence are scrutinized to avoid potential PR issues.

3. Situational Judgment Tests (SJTs): These tests present players with hypothetical scenarios to gauge their decision-making and ethical reasoning.

The Importance of Behavioral Assessment Data

Behavioral data is important because it should symbolize an individual's intrinsic beliefs. Behavior is how we experience people every single day. In professional football, specific behavioral attributes are essential to perform well throughout a long and intense season.

John Harbaugh, head coach of the Baltimore Ravens, emphasizes the importance of character: "We want tough, smart, disciplined football players who love to play the game and have a passion for winning."[2]

Cultural Fit
1. Team cohesion: Behavioral data helps teams predict how well a player will integrate into their existing culture.
2. Leadership potential: Teams identify players who can step into leadership roles and positively influence the locker room.

Predicting Future Behavior
1. Risk management: Behavioral assessments help teams identify potential red flags and manage risk in their talent acquisitions.
2. Long-term success: Teams use this data to predict a player's ability to adapt and thrive in the NFL environment over time.

Integrating Data into the Decision-Making Process

Kevin Colbert, former general manager of the Pittsburgh Steelers, explains their approach: "We try to blend the analytics with the scouting to come up with the best decision possible."

Data Synthesis

1. Cross-referencing data points: Teams create comprehensive player profiles by combining performance metrics with psychological and behavioral data.
2. Weighting factors: Different data points are prioritized based on positional needs and team-specific criteria.

Predictive Modeling

1. Data analytics teams: Many NFL franchises now employ data scientists to build sophisticated predictive models for player success.
2. Scenario planning: Teams use data-driven simulations to project how a player might perform in various situations or develop over time.

The integration of performance metrics, psychological assessments, and behavioral data has transformed NFL talent acquisition. As teams continue to refine their processes, the ability to effectively analyze and apply this wealth of information will be crucial in building championship-caliber rosters.

This strategy is crucial in building and sustaining your organizational culture. Just as NFL teams go above and beyond to ensure that their investments work, how can we apply the same level of analysis in our organizations that empower our talent decision-making process, elevate our ability to coach and develop company team members, and ensure we are hiring toward natural culture alignment?

The NFL's data-driven approach to talent acquisition and development has revolutionized the sport, leading to more precise player selection and improved team performance. This methodology is not limited to the realm of professional sports; it can be effectively applied to corporate environments, yielding similar benefits in hiring, employee development, and organizational culture.

After reading Geno Wickman's book *The EOS Life*, which describes his company, the Entrepreneurial Operating System, I had a lightbulb moment. Has anyone ever created something similar but with a focus on culture being the primary strategy of the company? It hadn't been done, so I did it. I launched "COS," the *Culture Operating Strategy*.

During that process I also became a small partner in a profound behavioral assessment company, founded by my friend and assessment mentor, Rick Breden. In 2006 Rick set out to change how we apply behavioral science data. The mission of our behavioral assessment is to enhance individual and organizational success by aligning behavioral tendencies with roles and corporate cultures.

At the core of my Culture Operating Strategy methodology is the E3 Behavioral Insights Platform, a comprehensive behavioral profiling tool that evaluates 21 behavioral scales, offering a nuanced understanding of a person's strengths and areas for growth.

The E3 Assessment goes beyond traditional personality tests by recognizing that behaviors can be developed and refined over time. This approach aligns with the perspective of renowned organizational psychologist Adam Grant, who states, "The hallmark of originality is rejecting the default and exploring whether a better option exists."[3]

By providing a more dynamic view of individual potential, the E3 Assessment opens up new possibilities for personal and professional growth.

Applications in the Corporate World

In the corporate world, this behavioral data can be applied in three ways that mirror NFL strategies: enhancing hiring with behavioral data, human development and coaching, and benchmarking role and culture behaviors.

Enhancing Hiring with Behavioral Data

Just as NFL teams create profiles of successful players for specific positions, companies can use data from top-performing employees to create benchmarks for specific roles. This ensures a good fit for both the role and the company culture. Recall my earlier belief (see Chapter 4) that challenges Peter Drucker's famous culture quote: When Culture is the strategy, it eats every meal at every time of the day. By aligning new hires with the existing culture, companies can maintain their strategic direction and values.

Human Development and Coaching

NFL teams use psychological data to develop players' skills and mindset. Similarly, companies can use behavioral assessment data to create personalized coaching reports and development plans. This approach resonates with the philosophy of leadership expert John C. Maxwell, who asserts, "The greatest leader is willing to train people and develop them to the point that they eventually surpass him or her in knowledge and ability."[4]

Benchmarking Role and Culture Behaviors

Beyond individual roles, behavioral data can be used to align candidates and employees with the company's core beliefs, values, and culture. This is crucial for building a strong, cohesive organizational culture where employees feel connected to the company's mission and vision. As Simon Sinek, author and organizational consultant, puts it, "Customers will never love a company until the employees love it first."[5]

The application of behavioral data in corporate settings is not without its challenges. It requires a commitment to data-driven decision-making and a willingness to invest in employee development. However, the potential benefits are substantial. Companies that effectively leverage behavioral data can create more engaged workforces, develop stronger leaders, and sustain cultures that drive long-term success.

As we continue to learn from the successes of data application in professional sports, it's clear that the corporate world has much to gain from adopting similar strategies. By understanding and aligning individual beliefs and behaviors with organizational needs, companies can create environments where employees thrive, leading to improved performance and sustainable success.

When all is said and done, after you have utilized all of the data to make better decisions, after the game was won or lost, after you achieved or missed your work goals, culture exists, whether you believe in it or not. Culture is always there and its significance is found in one powerful pursuit: purpose!

13

Purpose

ALL I REMEMBER is the heavy, controlled breathing. "Huuuuugh—whoooo. Huuuuugh—whoooo." Lying in bed next to my wife, my entire life was about to change. "Babe, are you okay? What's going on?"

She looked at me with total assurance and said, "Contractions. It's time!" Now, dads, you'll all relate to this exact moment. As a professional football player, I had dedicated my life to the importance of practice and preparation. Believe me, we practiced this exact "play" so many times I could perform it in my sleep.

Pack the hospital bag, set out the outfits, prepare the "pregnancy playlist," call the support team. Breathe! Never stop coaching her on breathing technique. Get to the car safely, drive safely, park safely. Enter the correct hospital door, find the right check-in desk. Oh my gosh, I want to cry out a stress-scream as I relive that experience. Then the moment actually came, and all of that practice and preparation flew out the door. I couldn't remember a single step. I was running around the house like a headless chicken, trying to organize my thoughts into a single doable action that would help her.

Hours later, in the early morning of my wife's birthday, March 1, 2009, Karyn began to push. I was right beside her the entire time, encouraging this champion of a woman. Our hands locked in a life-long commitment grip as I watched everything with eyes wide open. I had made a commitment to witness my children coming into this world, and there was no way I was backing out now.

Karyn's OBGYN looked at me and asked, "Are you ready?" Pale-faced, I looked back at her and said, "Let's go." The physician began coaching Karyn, "You're doing great. Give me your strongest push in 3...2...1—push!" As I looked down, I couldn't believe my eyes as I watched this beautiful new face enter the world. The physician said again, "One more big push, Karyn. You can do it, 3...2...1—push!" And just like that, Elleora Grace Utecht was born. I could hardly hold it together, but I had to because I played a critical role in the upcoming minutes: cutting the umbilical cord. That was such a special moment because it completely separated Elleora from the womb and solidified her existence in the world.

As I held her in my arms for the first time, I became overwhelmed with emotion, and my 6-foot 7-inch, 255-pound frame just crumbled inside, into a pool of unconditional love. That was the moment the purpose of my life forever changed. My significance and value as a man and husband instantly transformed into a purpose-driven father.

Becoming a parent taught me how important discovering the what and why of my purpose was. Even more essential, it challenged me on how I was going to practice behavior that deeply reflected my purpose.

When culture is chosen and developed into an objective strategy that drives system performance, it should create and foster a workplace environment that empowers all team members to identify and capture their purpose as humans, leaders, and employees. John C. Maxwell says, "Leaders aren't born, they are made."[1] This powerful truth means all humans on the planet are capable of being leaders. They have a purpose that reveals their significance and value. Imagine if the strategy of every executive leadership team was to accomplish the goal of empowering the human condition of their entire team to discover, develop, and direct their purpose toward life and business.

Not only will you enhance workplace performance and expand growth and profit but, more importantly, you will transform your people into the best versions of themselves. That, my friends, is a corporate legacy worth having pride in.

There is no better example to learn about purpose than from Pastor Rick Warren's book *The Purpose Driven Life*. Rick's book hit a nerve and is radically powerful, and not only for people of faith. This is why *The Purpose Driven Life* has sold over 50 million copies worldwide!

Rick Warren chose to practice a nonnegotiable belief he was committed to—to give away the majority of the book's earnings. When speaking about his own purpose, Rick shared that he has given 90% of his book sales to various charities and causes, especially those focusing on poverty, health, and education. That, my friends, is a life on purpose!

Let's take a closer look at the impact of *The Purpose Driven Life* and what lessons we can learn from it.

Practicing a Culture of Purpose

Rick Warren eloquently states, "Without God, life has no purpose, and without purpose, life has no meaning."[2] This profound insight sets the stage for understanding the transformative power of purpose in our lives and organizations. Remember, I am a pastor's kid, so I like to bring in organizational insights from many platforms, including religion.

When you read comments that contain faith language, please look at them through the lens of objective application, not evangelism. There is so much fruit to be consumed if you're willing to explore all forms of wisdom. Let's pursue how we can cultivate a culture of purpose in our personal and professional spheres.

Understanding Purpose

Purpose, as Warren defines it, is the reason for which something exists or is done. He emphasizes, "You were made by God and for God." Another way of understanding would be for a purpose much bigger than yourself, "and until you understand that, life will never make sense."[3] This perspective shifts our focus from self-centered goals to a higher calling, encouraging us to align our actions with a greater purpose.

In the workplace, understanding purpose means recognizing that our roles contribute to something larger than ourselves. It's about seeing how our daily tasks, no matter how small, fit into the bigger picture of the organization's mission and impact on society.

The Importance of Knowing Your Purpose

Warren asserts, "Knowing your purpose gives meaning to your life."[4] When we understand our purpose, it acts as a compass, guiding our decisions and actions. In the corporate world, this translates to employees who are more engaged, motivated, and resilient in the face of challenges.

As leaders, fostering an environment where individuals can discover and live out their purpose can lead to a more vibrant and productive workplace. Warren reminds us, "We are products of our past, but we don't have to be prisoners of it." This encourages a growth mindset and the belief that everyone can find and fulfill their purpose.

The Transformative Power of Living Out Your Purpose

Living with purpose has a ripple effect that extends far beyond the individual. Warren states, "When you live on purpose, your actions have eternal consequences."[5] In the context of organizational culture, this means that purpose-driven employees not only perform better but also inspire and uplift those around them.

By cultivating a culture of purpose, we create an environment where people are not just working for a paycheck, but are invested in a shared belief strategy, vision, and mission. This leads to increased innovation, collaboration, and overall job satisfaction. Let's take a look at two strategies that can be practiced to enhance a culture of purpose.

Discovering and Practicing Purpose in the Workplace to Improve Corporate Culture

To foster a purpose-driven culture, organizations can facilitate workshops and discussions about personal and organizational purpose.

- Align individual roles with the company's broader mission.
- Recognize and celebrate purpose-driven behaviors and achievements.
- Provide opportunities for employees to contribute to meaningful projects beyond their job descriptions.
- Encourage mentorship programs that help individuals explore and develop their sense of purpose.

I believe Warren's insights translate into the workplace by helping employees see how their work contributes to the greater good and aligns with their personal beliefs and values.

Practicing Purpose in Life to Transform Relationships

In our personal lives, living with purpose can dramatically improve our relationships. Warren teaches, "Life is meant to be shared."[6] To practice purpose in relationships:

- Identify your core beliefs and values and how they manifest in your interactions with others.
- Seek to understand and support the purposes of those around you.
- Communicate openly about your performance goals and aspirations, and encourage others to do the same.
- Invest time and energy in relationships that align with your purpose, beliefs, and values.
- Practice active listening and empathy to deepen connections.

Warren reminds us, "You were made for a mission."[7] By living out our purpose in relationships, we not only enrich our own lives but also inspire and uplift those around us.

I was sitting in my office at home in the spring of 2019 when the call came. When I answered I was surprised to hear a familiar voice. "Hi Ben, it's Coach Dungy."

"Hey Coach, great to hear your voice, it's been a while." It really was great to hear his voice. He played such a major role in my life and because of him I am living out my passion today for culture and people transformation.

I asked, "What's going on?" His answer sent humble goose bumps all across my body. Dungy preceded to tell me that after much prayer and thoughtful consideration, he and his wife, Lauren, had decided I would be the recipient of his prestigious "Uncommon Leader Award," which is given to an individual in professional sports who displays exceptional leadership both on and off the field.

Here are coach Dungy's words as he describes what it means to be an "Uncommon Leader":

The mandate to be Uncommon actually came to me from three different sources. The first was my dad. When I was growing up, he always talked to us about not following the crowd and not doing something just because everyone else was doing it. He encouraged us to chase our own dreams, even if it meant being ridiculed for being different.

When I arrived at the University of Minnesota as a freshman football player, "Former" coach, Cal Stoll, built upon my dad's theme. He said, "Success is uncommon, therefore not to be enjoyed by the common man." He was looking for men who had the attitude and desire to do what everyone else could do, but most people wouldn't.

The third, and most important source of the Uncommon idea was the Bible. One of my mom's favorite scriptures was Matthew 7:13–14, where Jesus talks about entering through the narrow gate and traveling the narrow path rather than the broad highway. He was talking about salvation and the way to heaven, but I think it applies to life as well.

We should never be afraid to take the tough road, to follow a higher calling, or set a higher standard. In short, we should never be satisfied with being average, but should strive to be Uncommon.[8]

I was completely blown away and humbled by this honor. This award had previously gone to extraordinary people like NFL football anchor James Brown and my Hall of Fame quarterback Peyton Manning. The first thoughts that entered my mind were "This must be a mistake. I am not worthy of this award. I don't have the performance accolades praiseworthy enough to be included."

Coach Dungy must have felt what I was feeling because he immediately explained that this award is not about achievements or trophies. It's not about financial successes or performance statistics. It is about the leadership quality of a man.

He continued by affirming my life, behavior, and faith as an athlete on and off the field, and my focus and commitment to being a strong husband, father, and friend. He thanked me for being "Uncommon."

As I walked out of my office calling for my wife to share the news, all I could do was crumble to the floor with emotion.

The "Uncommon Award" reception was so special for my family and friends, and the entire experience gave my life a new level of purpose. I committed to wake up every morning and make the choice to live in an uncommon way, using my beliefs and values to positively impact the lives of all those I come in contact with.

Not to mention the award itself was unbelievable. A massive 85-pound iron trophy now sits in my office featuring metal silhouettes of the three most impactful men in Coach Dungy's life: his father, Coach Cal Stoll, and Martin Luther King Jr, with the engraving "Uncommon Leader Award."

Embracing and practicing a culture of purpose, both in our personal lives and in the workplace, has the power to transform individuals, relationships, and entire organizations. As Rick Warren wisely states, "What matters is not the duration of your life, but the donation of it."[9] By aligning our actions with our purpose, we create a legacy of positive impact and fulfillment that extends far beyond ourselves.

Let us strive to create environments where purpose flourishes, where individuals are empowered to discover their unique contributions, and where collective efforts are directed toward meaningful goals. In doing so, we not only enhance our own lives but also contribute to a more purposeful and harmonious world.

14

My NFL Miracle

As I REFLECT on my journey to the NFL, I'm reminded of a profound truth: miracles happen every day. My story is a testament to this, and it all began with a chance encounter that would change the course of my life.

Two months after my senior year at the University of Minnesota, I found myself sharing the stage with Coach Tony Dungy at an Athletes in Action Alumni banquet. Coach Dungy, a fellow U of MN alum and future Hall of Fame coach, was the keynote speaker. I was there to open for him as a speaker, still recovering from a severe abdominal injury and uncertain about my future in football.

Have you ever been in a life situation where everything you have worked for could disappear? That is exactly where I was. As an All-Big Ten Tight End, preseason All-American, and a Mackey Award candidate for the Nation's top Tight End, I was now questioning whether I would even be chosen by an NFL team because of my injury.

Standing before 500–600 people, I mustered up the courage to break the ice with a joke: "Us alumni stick together. I expect that a U of MN alumni like yourself is going to draft me because we come from the same family." The crowd laughed, and Coach Dungy smiled. Little did I know how prophetic those words would become.

When Coach Dungy took the stage, his first words resonated deeply with me: "We are family. We do stick together. Unfortunately we drafted a tight end in the first round last year so your position will not be a priority for us in the draft this year." Then he paused and backed away from the podium and placed his hand on his chin as though he was receiving information from a much higher source. He came back to the podium, addressing me directly in front of the entire audience, he said something that would stay with me for years to come:

"Ben, if for some reason you slip through the cracks, which I can't see happening, I promise you that I'll be the first person to call."

At the time, I couldn't have imagined how significant that promise would become. As Simon Sinek, a leader in organizational culture, often says, "People don't buy what you do; they buy why you do it."[1] Coach Dungy's "why" was clear: He believed in the power of integrity, family, loyalty, and keeping his word.

The draft came and went, and to my dismay, even though I was one of the top tight ends in the country and projected to be a potential first-round pick, I wasn't selected. It was an embarrassing, humbling, and devastating experience. I felt lost, my dreams of playing in the NFL slipping away. But as Patrick Lencioni, author of *The Five Dysfunctions of a Team*, reminds us, "If you're not willing to accept that most of what we do in life takes perseverance, then you're going to have a hard time being successful. But if you are willing to embrace the idea that hard work, patience, and dedication are required, you'll be well on your way to achieving great things, especially in building a cohesive team."[2]

In that moment of vulnerability, surrounded by my family and agent, I learned the true meaning of resilience. And then, just seconds after the free agent market opened, a miracle happened. The phone in the middle of my agent's desk rang, and on the other end was none other than Coach Tony Dungy and Bill Polian, the general manager of the Indianapolis Colts. The fact that the head coach and the general manager were calling me as a free agent was significant. It made me feel like I mattered and had value.

Coach Dungy's words still fills me with pure joy: "Listen, we know how talented you are and how great a tight end you can be when you're healthy. We've also had experience with your specific abdominal injury. We know what to do and who to send you to."

In hearing Coach Dungy's words, I witnessed firsthand the power of integrity and character. Coach Dungy had kept his promise, demonstrating what true leadership looks like. As Simon Sinek says, "Leadership is not about being in charge. Leadership is about taking care of those in your charge."[3]

The Colts offered me not just a contract, but a chance to heal and prove myself. They invested in me when I had nothing to offer in return. This act of faith taught me a valuable lesson about organizational culture: when leaders live their beliefs and values, they create an environment where miracles can happen.

My journey with the Colts wasn't easy. I underwent surgery, faced a long recovery, and had to fight my way back to top form. But through it all, I was supported by a team that believed in me. Another Lencioni belief states, "The single biggest advantage any company can achieve is organizational health. Yet it is ignored by most leaders even though it is simple, free, and available to anyone who wants it."[4]

Three years later, I found myself on the field as a starting tight end in the Super Bowl. From undrafted free agent to world champion, my journey was a testament to the power of perseverance, faith, and the impact of a positive organizational culture.

As I shared earlier in the book we have the only Super Bowl ring in the history of the NFL to have one of our team beliefs engraved in the side of our ring, and it's the word "Faith." It was symbolic, not of religion, but of the power of trust and hope.

The acronym for that word on our team was Freedom for All Individuals to Trust and Hope in each other.

Coach Dungy was able to build a F.A.M.I.L.Y. (Forget About Me, I Love You) who trusted and hoped in each other out of 53 of the most diverse, talented, and driven men in the country. That is a champion success story in itself.

This experience taught me invaluable lessons about life and leadership. I learned that you can't control everything, but you can control your attitude and effort. As Simon Sinek advises, "The goal is not to be perfect by the end. The goal is to be better today."[5]

I also learned the importance of approaching life with open hands, ready to pour your heart into your passions while remaining flexible to unexpected opportunities. This mindset gives you the freedom to prepare without trying to outguess the outcome.

My NFL miracle story is a reminder that when we practice our beliefs and values, we can positively change people's lives. It's about creating a culture of trust, integrity, and mutual support. A final word from Patrick Lencioni says, "The true measure of a team is not whether it accomplishes what it sets out to achieve, but whether it can break through and transcend the boundaries of achievement to enter the realm of greatness."[6]

Today, as I share my story, I'm reminded of the ripple effect of kindness and integrity. Coach Dungy's decision to honor his word didn't just impact my life; it set in motion a series of events that led to a Super Bowl victory and beyond. It's a testament to the fact that when we practice our beliefs and values, and create a culture of support and excellence, we can achieve the impossible.

As you face your own challenges and pursue your dreams, remember that miracles do happen. They often come disguised as unexpected phone calls, second chances, or people who believe in you when you've stopped believing in yourself. Embrace these moments, and never underestimate the power of a promise kept.

In the words of Simon Sinek, "Working hard for something we don't care about is called stress. Working hard for something we love is called passion."[7] Find your passion, surround yourself with people who believe in you, and create a culture where miracles can thrive. Because in the end, it's not just about winning games or achieving personal success—it's about the lives we touch and the legacy we leave behind.

My journey from undrafted free agent to Super Bowl champion is a testament to the power of culture, integrity, and perseverance. It's a reminder that when we practice what we preach and surround ourselves with people who share our beliefs and values, we can overcome any obstacle and achieve greatness.

So, as you pursue your own dreams, remember that miracles do happen, often when we least expect them. Stay true to your beliefs and values, keep your promises, and always be ready for that life-changing phone call. You never know when your own NFL miracle might be just around the corner.

That miracle taught me the most important part of building a championship organizational culture. Culture is the human condition at work, and people are the most vital asset within every organization. Dungy and the "Colts Way" culture unveiled a powerful truth. When you make culture your central corporate strategy and apply systems to practice it, not only can you win a world championship in business, but more importantly your culture will transform its people. Make your culture their miracle!

BELIEVE in the CHAMPION'S CREED!

Afterword

On February 4, 2007, it seemed quite natural to me as Ben's dad to continue a tradition of connecting with Ben in preparation for a contest. Just prior to the start of his playing in Super Bowl XLI I felt compelled to make my way to a position in the Miami Dolphins Stadium where, for one more time, the two of us could exchange that glance of love and support that characterized our relationship.

I mentioned to my wife, Lori, that I wanted to say hi to Ben and let him know we were there rooting for him in this mega football venue seen around the world. Our seats were on the 20-yard line around 10 rows up near the entrance where the Colts would take the field. Thus, I rose from my seat and carefully, as quickly as possible, strode around the end-zone concourse to the tunnel, midpoint between the hash marks, where I knew the team would enter the arena.

Many of the players jogged on the field in sync with others who also played their position. It didn't take long to recognize a couple of tight-end position players coming onto the field and so I anticipated Ben would follow soon after. I was so excited to let him know we were near, poised to lift him up with prayers for strength, humility, safety, and joy.

As he ran through the tunnel on route to the playing field, I shouted his name: "Ben, Ben!" There was no response. "Did he hear me?" I figured the crowd noise must have been pretty high on the decibel count since he seemed oblivious to my call. So I shouted again: "Ben! Benjamin!!" It was then he stopped, turned, and paused with a quizzical look on his face that quickly gave way to a heartening smile. Then Ben put his hand up as if to say, "Sorry, Dad, not now. I've got to get to work." But at least I was able to make that fatherly connection with my son.

I began my journey back to my seat, when all of a sudden I heard a voice shouting, "Dad! Dad!" Ben hurried back toward the tunnel entrance, reached up, and caught my hand as I leaned over the guardrail. I assured him we were cheering him on in love and faith. He acknowledged the same, saying, "Dad, it all started with you in the backyard. I love you." Pride and hope welled up in my heart to new heights. Years of believing and loving, patience, and practice found fulfillment in tears of joy. "Go out and play your game. Do the best you can with what you've got, whatever the play or situation, in every opportunity God gives you."

We never dreamed we would attend a Super Bowl football game, let alone one in which our son would be a competitor. For 25-plus years Lori and I had watched and encouraged our son Ben as he grew through the challenges and adventures of the "sporting life" with an absorbing determination to be the best. Each passing year ended with a growing sense of accomplishment, perhaps destiny, for this highly motivated and enthused athlete.

As a youngster, Ben gave almost every sport a fair chance to capture his heart. Swimming, diving, wrestling, baseball, soccer, basketball, track and field, hockey, and of course, football. Though he was talented at all of these, it was the last two that became his passion and joy. He simply could not hold back his competitive fire and pureness of joy when the game would begin.

I admired his belief in self, his love for sport along with a jubilant nature to win, and his sheer desire to excel. I determined early on to be and do what I could to support and encourage his interest and development in sport and faith and life. As a family, we all had such great fun being a part of Ben's journey.

In Ben's high school years, there was many an afternoon I stopped by the field or the ice rink to observe his practices for a half hour or so. We always shared a glance, a smile, a nod, a wave, an awareness of presence, support, and love. Similar expressions accompanied every activity or game we attended. It was commonplace for us as a family to simply convey assurance, care, and encouragement through physical gestures from afar.

In all the time Ben played sports I rarely missed a game, whether watching in person or via television. Before each game Ben often asked his mom and me to pray for him (he would call us on the phone in college or as a pro) and we readily did so, citing a scripture, voicing our love for him and the belief that he would do well. Sometimes I reminded him, "Remember, as much as you are better than some, there are always others who are better than you. That's okay. That's life. So don't get caught up in comparisons. Just go out and play your game. Do the best you can with what you've got, whatever the play or situation, in every opportunity God gives you." And with eyes as big as saucers he embraced it all.

Over the ensuing years since football, Ben has continued to approach life with the same passion and belief in the principles of hard work, goal-setting (keep your eye on the prize), accountability and trust within relationships (we need each other to achieve a desired outcome), and self-discipline. He has come to model an internal steadiness and peace, no matter the circumstances.

Of course, there are always challenges, disappointments, and drawbacks along the path to success (joy). But maintaining one's belief in self, others, and the principles that shape behavior for the good will allow us to thrive. That is now the code that defines Ben Utecht.

Ben's grandfather and my dad, Bob Utecht, the great rink-side announcer for the Minnesota North Stars, would add this thought on both sport and life: "The joy is in the journey—'nough said!"

—Jeff Utecht

Notes

Chapter 2

1. Edgar H. Schein, *Organizational Culture and Leadership* (San Francisco: Jossey-Bass, 2010), 74.
2. John C. Maxwell, *Developing the Leader Within You* (Nashville: Thomas Nelson, 1993), 29.
3. Personal communication with Dr. Daniel Zismer, 2017.
4. Schein, *Organizational Culture and Leadership*.
5. Maxwell, *Leadership Gold: Lessons I've Learned from a Lifetime of Leading* (Nashville: Thomas Nelson, 2008), 37.
6. Personal communication with Dr. Daniel Zismer, 2017.
7. Schein, *Organizational Culture and Leadership*.
8. Maxwell, *Developing the Leader Within You*, 128.

Chapter 3

1. Edgar H. Schein, *Organizational Culture and Leadership* (San Francisco: Jossey-Bass, 1985), 9.

2. John C. Maxwell, *The 21 Irrefutable Laws of Leadership: Follow Them and People Will Follow You* (Nashville: Thomas Nelson, 1998), 30.
3. Personal communication with Dr. Daniel Zismer, 2017.
4. John C. Maxwell, *Leadership Gold: Lessons I've Learned from a Lifetime of Leading* (Nashville: Thomas Nelson, 2008), 19.
5. Personal communication with Dr. Daniel Zismer, 2017.

Chapter 4

1. Edgar H. Schein, *Organizational Culture and Leadership* (San Francisco: Jossey-Bass, 1985), 2.
2. Kim S. Cameron and Robert E. Quinn, *Diagnosing and Changing Organizational Culture: Based on the Competing Values Framework* (Reading, MA: Addison-Wesley, 1999), 10.
3. John P. Kotter, *Leading Change* (Boston: Harvard Business Review Press, 1996), 148.
4. Daniel R. Denison and Aneil K. Mishra, "Toward a Theory of Organizational Culture and Effectiveness," *Organization Science* 6, no. 2 (1995): 215.
5. Ibid., 215.
6. Bain & Company, *The Focused Organization: How to Win the "20/20" Customer* (Boston: Bain & Company, 2018), 12.

Chapter 5

1. Ken Blanchard and Phil Hodges, *Lead Like Jesus: Lessons from the Greatest Leadership Role Model of All Time* (Nashville: Thomas Nelson, 2005), 21.
2. Rodney Stark, *The Rise of Christianity: How the Obscure, Marginal Jesus Movement Became the Dominant Religious Force* (San Francisco: HarperSanFrancisco, 1997), 209.
3. Tony Bridwell, *The Kingmaker: A Leadership Story of Integrity and Purpose* (Dallas: Clovercroft Publishing, 2016), 45.

4. Personal communication with Dr. Tony Bridwell, 2024.
5. Bridwell, *The Kingmaker*, 72.
6. Ibid., 88.

Chapter 6

1. Personal communication with Michael Brennan, 2024.
2. Northwestern Mutual, "Our Beliefs," *Northwestern Mutual*, accessed September 18, 2024 https://www.northwesternmutual.com/who-we-are/

Chapter 7

1. Tony Dungy, *Quiet Strength: The Principles, Practices, and Priorities of a Winning Life* (Carol Stream, IL: Tyndale House Publishers, 2007), 185.
2. Tony Dungy, *Uncommon: Finding Your Path to Significance* (Carol Stream, IL: Tyndale House Publishers, 2009), 85.
3. Dungy, *Uncommon*, 102.
4. Dungy, *Quiet Strength*, 143.
5. Ibid., 185.
6. Dungy, *Uncommon*, 45.

Chapter 8

1. Edgar H. Schein, *Organizational Culture and Leadership* (San Francisco: Jossey-Bass, 1985), 2.
2. *Dictionary.com*, s.v. "integrity," accessed June 21, 2022, https://www.dictionary.com/browse/integrity.

Chapter 9

1. Gino Wickman, *Traction: Get a Grip on Your Business* (Dallas: Ben-Bella Books, 2012), 57.
2. Will Guidara, *Unreasonable Hospitality: The Remarkable Power of Giving People More Than They Expect* (New York: Optimism Press, 2022), 105.
3. Vince Lombardi, quoted in *Vince Lombardi on Leadership: Life Lessons from a Five-Time NFL Championship Coach*, by Pat Williams with James Denney (Avon, MA: Adams Media, 2001), 45.
4. Bill Belichick, quoted in *Belichick and Brady: Two Men, the Patriots, and How They Revolutionized Football*, by Michael Holley (New York: Hachette Books, 2016), 63.
5. *Merriam-webster.com*, s.v. "integrality," accessed November 8, 2024, https://www.merriam-webster.com/dictionary/integral.
6. Tom Landry, quoted in *Leadership Lessons of the Navy SEALs: Battle-Tested Strategies for Creating Successful Organizations and Inspiring Extraordinary Results*, by Jeff Cannon and Jon Cannon (New York: McGraw-Hill, 2005), 83.
7. Tony Dungy, *The Mentor Leader: Secrets to Building People and Teams That Win Consistently* (Carol Stream, IL: Tyndale House Publishers, 2010), 12.

Chapter 10

1. Edgar H. Schein, *Organizational Culture and Leadership* (San Francisco: Jossey-Bass, 1985), 236.
2. Jim Collins, *Good to Great: Why Some Companies Make the Leap ... and Others Don't* (New York: HarperCollins, 2001), 140.
3. Adam Grant, *Originals: How Non-Conformists Move the World* (New York: Viking, 2016), 91.

Chapter 11

1. Tom Brady, quoted in *The TB12 Method: How to Achieve a Lifetime of Sustained Peak Performance* (New York: Simon & Schuster, 2017), 132.

2. Jack Welch, *Jack: Straight from the Gut* (New York: Warner Books, 2001), 284.

3. Warren Buffett, quoted in *The Essays of Warren Buffett: Lessons for Corporate America*, ed. Lawrence A. Cunningham (Cardozo Law Review, 1997), 94.

4. Phil Jackson, Sacred Hoops: *Spiritual Lessons of a Hardwood Warrior* (New York: Hyperion, 1995), 103.

5. John Wooden, *Wooden: A Lifetime of Observations and Reflections On and Off the Court* (New York: McGraw-Hill, 1997), 85.

Chapter 12

1. Bill Belichick, quoted in *Belichick: The Making of the Greatest Football Coach of All Time*, by Ian O'Connor (Boston: Houghton Mifflin Harcourt, 2018), 207.

2. John Harbaugh, quoted in *Earn the Right to Win: How Success in Any Field Starts with Superior Preparation*, by Tom Coughlin with David Fisher (New York: Penguin Publishing Group, 2013), 112.

3. Adam Grant, *Originals: How Non-Conformists Move the World* (New York: Viking, 2016), 3.

4. John C. Maxwell, *The 5 Levels of Leadership: Proven Steps to Maximize Your Potential* (New York: Center Street, 2011), 87.

5. Simon Sinek, *Leaders Eat Last: Why Some Teams Pull Together and Others Don't* (New York: Portfolio, 2014), 85.

Chapter 13

1. John C. Maxwell, *Developing the Leader Within You* (Nashville: Thomas Nelson, 1993), 1.

2. Rick Warren, *The Purpose Driven Life: What on Earth Am I Here For?* (Grand Rapids, MI: Zondervan, 2002), 17.
3. Ibid., 25.
4. Ibid., 30.
5. Ibid., 43.
6. Ibid., 125.
7. Ibid., 281.
8. AriseWithTheGuys.com "Uncommon Award" accessed November 9, 2024 https://www.arisewiththeguys.com.
9. Warren, *The Purpose Driven Life*, 233.

Chapter 14

1. Simon Sinek, *Start with Why: How Great Leaders Inspire Everyone to Take Action* (New York: Portfolio, 2009), 39.
2. Patrick Lencioni, *The Five Dysfunctions of a Team: A Leadership Fable* (San Francisco: Jossey-Bass, 2002), 210.
3. Simon Sinek, *Leaders Eat Last: Why Some Teams Pull Together and Others Don't* (New York: Portfolio, 2014), 23.
4. Patrick Lencioni, *The Advantage: Why Organizational Health Trumps Everything Else in Business* (San Francisco: Jossey-Bass, 2012), 1.
5. Sinek, *Start with Why*, 98.
6. Lencioni, *The Five Dysfunctions of a Team*, 190.
7. Sinek, *Leaders Eat Last*, 74.

Acknowledgments

FIRST AND FOREMOST, to my incredible wife, Karyn, your love, strength, and leadership have been my compass through the storms of life. I am endlessly grateful for your partnership, which has made every triumph and challenge more meaningful.

To my four daughters—Elleora, Katriel, Amy, and Haven—your light fills my world with joy beyond measure. You are my daily inspiration and the reason I strive to be my very best.

I want to thank my parents, Jeff and Lori Utecht, whose unconditional love and unwavering support allowed me to pursue my dreams with confidence. Your belief in me has been the foundation of everything I've achieved.

A heartfelt thank-you to my Head Coach, Tony Dungy, and the entire Indianapolis Colts organization. You instilled in me the values of teamwork, perseverance, and a culture of excellence that have shaped my journey far beyond the field.

To my culture and business mentors—Dr. Tony Bridwell, Dr. Kent Myers, Scott Hillstrom, Mario Nozzarella, Jaime Taets,

133

Dr. Daniel Zismer, and my 8 Streams of Influence leadership group—your wisdom and guidance have profoundly impacted my understanding of leadership and organizational culture. I am blessed to have learned from you.

I am also deeply thankful to those who have provided their endorsements and encouragement: John C. Maxwell, David Horsager, DeMaurice Smith, Dr. Tony Bridwell, Jaime Taets, and Jon Gordon. Your words and support have added immense value to this project.

To all the companies and teams featured in this book, it has been a privilege to work alongside you and to witness your commitment to building extraordinary cultures. Your stories have made this book truly transformational.

Finally, I extend my deepest gratitude to Wiley Publishing for bringing *The Champion's Creed* to life. Your partnership has made it possible to share this message of leadership, culture, and resilience with the world.

Thank you all for being a part of this journey—it has been one of the greatest honors of my life.

About the Author

Experience a commanding corporate presence that inspires, teaches, and coaches on building a world championship organizational culture with Ben Utecht. Standing at 6 foot 7 inches and weighing 250 pounds, Ben is not only an NFL Super Bowl Champion tight end but also the chief culture officer who received the esteemed "Uncommon Leader Award" from NFL Hall of Fame Coach Tony Dungy for his exceptional leadership performance on and off the field. After retiring from football, Ben embarked on a remarkable career path, becoming a sought-after speaker for Fortune 500 companies, sharing his expertise in building high-performing cultures.

As the chief culture officer for True North Private Equity, overseeing a family of companies spanning multiple industries, Ben brings his passion for people and culture into corporate leadership. Additionally, he is culture and brand ambassador for Realty Group, an owner of Conquer Ninja Gyms, a top US Ninja

Fitness/Entertainment Franchise, and the founder of SoleCareRx, and the Culture Operating Strategy. To further enhance his impact on talent acquisition and leadership development, Ben became a partner in Behavioral Essentials, a technology company specializing in customized behavioral assessments and role and culture benchmarking.

Ben firmly believes that culture can be designed intentionally rather than left to chance. Empowering companies to define, create, implement, and lead culture strategies that drive bottom-line improvement while inspiring and developing individuals is his primary focus.

His philanthropic interests revolve around concussions, which abruptly ended his NFL career. Ben authored the compelling book *Counting the Days While My Mind Slips Away* in collaboration with Simon & Schuster and Howard Books, sharing his personal story of brain injury and the profound relationship between memory and relevance. Recognized as the spokesperson on concussion for the American Academy of Neurology, he received their prestigious Public Leadership in Neurology Award.

Beyond sports and leadership, Ben boasts a hidden talent as an award-nominated singer. With six albums under his belt, performances for presidents and symphonies, and even serenading Muhammad Ali on his birthday, his musical prowess captivates audiences. His viral YouTube hit, "You Will Always Be My Girls," touches hearts as it intertwines his concussion journey with his deep love for family. Ben truly embodies the essence of a modern-day Renaissance man.

Above all, Ben treasures the joy of sharing his life with his wife and four daughters.

Achievements:

2003 Team Captain, University of Minnesota

2003 First Team All Big Ten Tight End

2007 Super Bowl XLI Champion, Indianapolis Colts

2012 Dove Award Nominee

2013 Minnesota Brain Injury Alliance Ambassador Award

2014 Public Leadership in Neurology Award (American Academy of Neurology)

2019 Tony Dungy "Uncommon Leader" Award Winner

Index